ZECHARIAH

J. Vernon McGee

THOMAS NELSON
Since 1798

NASHVILLE DALLAS MEXICO CITY RIO DE JANEIRO

Published in Nashville, Tennessee, by Thomas Nelson, Inc.

Scripture quotations are from the KING JAMES VERSION of the Bible.

Library of Congress Cataloging-in-Publication Data

McGee, J. Vernon (John Vernon), 1904–1988
     [Thru the Bible with J. Vernon McGee]
     Thru the Bible commentary series / J. Vernon McGee.
          p.   cm.
     Reprint. Originally published: Thru the Bible with J. Vernon McGee. 1975.
     Includes bibliographical references.
     ISBN 0-7852-1035-0 (TR)
     ISBN 0-7852-1096-2 (NRM)
     1. Bible—Commentaries. I. Title.
BS491.2.M37   1991
220.7′7—dc20   90-41340
     ISBN: 978-0-7852-0606-4   CIP

Printed in the United States

HB 04.25.2024

CONTENTS

ZECHARIAH

PREFACE

The radio broadcasts of the Thru the Bible Radio five-year program were transcribed, edited, and published first in single-volume paperbacks to accommodate the radio audience.

There has been a minimal amount of further editing for this publication. Therefore, these messages are not the word-for-word recording of the taped messages which went out over the air. The changes were necessary to accommodate a reading audience rather than a listening audience.

These are popular messages, prepared originally for a radio audience. They should not be considered a commentary on the entire Bible in any sense of that term. These messages are devoid of any attempt to present a theological or technical commentary on the Bible. Behind these messages is a great deal of research and study in order to interpret the Bible from a popular rather than from a scholarly (and too-often boring) viewpoint.

We have definitely and deliberately attempted "to put the cookies on the bottom shelf so that the kiddies could get them."

The fact that these messages have been translated into many languages for radio broadcasting and have been received with enthusiasm reveals the need for a simple teaching of the whole Bible for the masses of the world.

I am indebted to many people and to many sources for bringing this volume into existence. I should express my especial thanks to my secretary, Gertrude Cutler, who supervised the editorial work; to Dr. Elliott R. Cole, my associate, who handled all the detailed work with the publishers; and finally, to my wife Ruth for tenaciously encouraging me from the beginning to put my notes and messages into printed form.

Solomon wrote, ". . . of making many books there is no end; and much study is a weariness of the flesh" (Eccl. 12:12). On a sea of books that flood the marketplace, we launch this series of THRU THE BIBLE with the hope that it might draw many to the one Book, *The Bible*.

J. VERNON MCGEE

The Book of
ZECHARIAH

INTRODUCTION

Zechariah, whose name means "whom Jehovah remembers," is identified as the son of Berechiah, which means "Jehovah blesses," and his father was the son of Iddo, which means "the appointed time." Certainly this cluster of names with such rich meanings is suggestive of the encouragement given to the remnant that had returned to Jerusalem after the Babylonian captivity—God remembers and blesses at the appointed time.

Although the name *Zechariah* was common among the Hebrew people (twenty-eight Zechariahs are mentioned in the Old Testament), there are Bible teachers who identify the Zechariah of this book with the "Zacharias" whom our Lord mentioned in Matthew 23:35 as having been martyred. Many expositors discount this possibility, but it is interesting to note that the Jewish Targum states that Zechariah was slain in the sanctuary and that he was both prophet and priest. In Nehemiah 12:4 Iddo is mentioned as one of the heads of a priestly family. And the historian "Josephus (*Wars*, iv. 5, 34) recounts the murder of a 'Zecharias, the son of Baruch,' i.e., Barachiah, as perpetrated in the Temple by the Zealots just before the destruction of Jerusalem" (*Ellicott's Commentary on the Whole Bible*).

Another interesting observation is that Zechariah's prophecy practically closes the Old Testament—it is next to the final book—and the New Testament opens chronologically with Luke's account of another *Zacharias* (meaning "Jehovah remembers") and his wife Elisabeth (meaning "His oath"). Zacharias was a priest who was serving at the altar of incense when an angel appeared to him with a message from

God after four hundred years of silence. So again God remembered His oath.

The prophecy was written in 520 B.C. Zechariah was contemporary with Haggai (see Ezra 5:1; 6:14), although he was probably a younger man (see Zech. 2:4).

This book has the characteristics of an apocalypse. The visions resemble those in the Books of Daniel and Ezekiel and Revelation. Daniel and Ezekiel were born in the land of Israel but wrote their books outside of it. Zechariah was born outside of the land down by the canals of Babylon, but he wrote in the land. It is interesting that Daniel, Ezekiel, and John were all outside Israel when they wrote. Only Zechariah was in that land when he wrote his apocalyptic visions. In the dark day of discouragement which blanketed the remnant, he saw the glory in all of the rapture and vision of hope. He has more messianic prophecies than any of the other minor prophets. This is therefore an important and interesting book.

Zechariah was contemporary with Haggai, but his book is in direct contrast to Haggai's. They definitely knew each other and prophesied to the same people at the same period of time. Yet their prophecies are just about as different as any two could be. They are literally ages apart even though they were given to the same people at the same time.

Haggai was down there at the foundation of the temple measuring it. He really had his feet on the ground. Zechariah was a man with his head in the air. Anyone who has ten visions in one night is doing pretty well! He was entirely visionary, whereas Haggai was entirely practical. Yet they were both speaking for God to the same people at the same time concerning the same problem. Also they both speak to us today, but each in his own manner.

We need to recognize that these two types of men are still needed today. They fit together. We need the practical, pragmatic man to go along with the man who is visionary because there is a danger in the dreamer. Too often the dreamers are not practical. On the other hand, the practical man so often lacks vision. So when you put these two together, you have a happy combination.

OUTLINE

Chapter 1

THEME: Apocalyptic visions: of riders under myrtle trees; of four horns; of four smiths

APOCALYPTIC VISIONS

The first six chapters are messianic and millennial. In this section is the record of ten visions, and Zechariah was given all of those ten visions in a single night. I would say that this was a good night's work, by the way!

INTRODUCTION AND MESSAGE OF WARNING

The first verse serves as an introduction to the Book of Zechariah.

> In the eighth month, in the second year of Darius, came the word of the Lord unto Zechariah, the son of Berechiah, the son of Iddo the prophet, saying [Zech. 1:1].

"In the eighth month, in the second year of Darius" gears this prophetic book into the reign of a gentile king because this is the period of the return of a remnant of Israel back to their land after the seventy-year captivity in Babylon. There is no king in either Israel or Judah now. The line of David is off the throne, and the Times of the Gentiles are in progress. "The second year of Darius" is the same year in which Haggai prophesied. They prophesied to the same people during the same period of time. Haggai began in the sixth month of that year, and Zechariah began two months later. It is the year 520 B.C. Haggai was given a prophecy in September, October, and December, but none in November. So this man Zechariah was given a prophecy in November, the month Haggai missed.

"Came the word of the Lord unto Zechariah." This is the same expression that Haggai used. In other words, Zechariah is speaking by the same authority that Haggai spoke. This same phrase occurs fourteen times in this book. Since the Book of Zechariah has fourteen chapters, it occurs on the average of once every chapter. As you can see, this is another book which places a great emphasis on the Word of God.

Now the second verse begins the message of warning which God has given Zechariah. Speaking by the same authority that Haggai did, the Word of the Lord, he is warning the returned remnant not to follow in the footsteps of their pre–Captivity fathers.

> **The LORD hath been sore displeased with your fathers [Zech. 1:2].**

Zechariah is telling them that the reason they had been in captivity was that "The LORD hath been sore displeased with your fathers." They had sinned against God, and he is warning them against making the same blunder, the same mistakes.

> **Therefore say thou unto them, Thus saith the LORD of hosts; Turn ye unto me, saith the LORD of hosts, and I will turn unto you, saith the LORD of hosts [Zech. 1:3].**

"Thus saith the LORD of hosts." That title for God has become almost a cliché for us; in fact many of the titles of God are almost meaningless to us, although we use them a great deal. What does "the LORD of hosts" really mean? It occurs fifty-two times in this book, which indicates its importance. The word *hosts* is derived from the Hebrew *tsaba* (plural: *tsabaoth*), meaning "service" or "strength" or even "warfare." The way it is used here "implies the boundless resources at His command for His people's good." That is Dr. Fausset's definition, and I can't improve on it. In the New Testament it says, "He is rich in mercy" (see Eph. 2:4), and "He has all power" (Matt. 28:18). So what do you need today, my friend? Do you need a little mercy? Well, he has an abundance of it. He is *rich* in it, and He can extend mercy to you. My, how we all need it! He is the Lord of Hosts—that title occurs three times in this verse and again in the fourth and sixth verses.

"Turn ye unto me, saith the LORD of hosts, and I will turn unto you." You see how He is extending mercy to them.

> **Be ye not as your fathers, unto whom the former prophets have cried, saying, Thus saith the LORD of hosts; Turn ye now from your evil ways, and from your evil doings: but they did not hear, nor hearken unto me, saith the LORD [Zech. 1:4].**

This is God's very practical warning. He is saying, "Your fathers paid no attention to the prophets whom I sent to them. I sent Hosea. I sent Joel. I sent Amos. I sent to them Isaiah and Jeremiah. I sent all of these prophets, but your fathers did not listen to them nor heed their message. That is the reason they went into captivity."

Now God asks a question—

> **Your fathers, where are they? and the prophets, do they live for ever? [Zech. 1:5].**

The voices of the former prophets are no longer sounding. Jeremiah and Isaiah and Hosea and Joel and Amos are gone. They are dead, and their voices are silent. And, by the way, "your fathers, where are they?" Well, they are buried down yonder in Babylon. That is the wrong place for an Israelite to be buried because he wants to be buried in his own land. Even old Jacob down in the land of Egypt made Joseph take an oath that he would not bury him there in Egypt. He said, "I want to be taken back up yonder and be buried with my fathers." And that is where his body is today—there in Hebron. The hope of the patriarchs and the godly Israelites was to be in their land at the time of the resurrection of the dead. If you have ever been to Jerusalem, you know that before the Eastern Gate, down through the Valley of Kidron and all up the side of the Mount of Olives are graves of Israelites. The Arabs mutilated a great many of them, but they are being restored by Israel. They want to be buried in that location because they expect to see the Messiah come to the earth at that place. And, personally, I believe that they will be raised from the dead when Christ returns to the earth to establish His Kingdom. Let me remind you that at the time of the Rapture the Lord Jesus will not come to the earth. Rather, He will call His own out of the earth and will meet them in the air. At that time He will not come to establish His Kingdom upon the earth. First the world will go through the Great Tribulation period, and then Christ will come to the earth to reign personally here. So you see that there would be no point in raising the Old Testament saints (both Jews and Gentiles) before the Tribulation because they would just have to stand around and wait until the Tribulation was over so that they could enter the Kingdom.

Therefore, you can see that God's question through Zechariah is very pertinent: "Your fathers, where are they?" They are buried down by the canals of Babylon, which is a bad place to be when your hope is in the land of Israel.

> But my words and my statutes, which I commanded my servants the prophets, did they not take hold of your fathers? and they returned and said, Like as the LORD of hosts thought to do unto us, according to our ways, and according to our doings, so hath he dealt with us [Zech. 1:6].

"Did they not take hold of your fathers?" means "did they not overtake your fathers?" The judgment for their sins overtook them.

"And they returned and said, Like as the LORD of hosts thought to do unto us, according to our ways, and according to our doings, so hath he dealt with us." They were finally willing to admit that the judgment which had come to them was just and righteous on the part of God—because He had warned them but they had not listened to Him.

This concludes the practical section. I don't mean that the next section is impractical; I simply mean that it deals with the visions which Zechariah had.

TEN VISIONS

While most expositors and commentators say that there are eight visions here, we will make a further division, as you will see.

VISION OF RIDERS UNDER MYRTLE TREES

The first vision is that of the horses and riders under the myrtle trees.

> **Upon the four and twentieth day of the eleventh month, which is the month Sebat, in the second year of Darius, came the word of the LORD unto Zechariah, the son of Berechiah, the son of Iddo the prophet, saying [Zech. 1:7].**

Since the Hebrew months do not begin with January, the eleventh month would be equivalent to our February—February 24, 520 B.C. We will see the significance of this in a few minutes.

Now let's get the background before us. Five months prior to this vision, the Lord had appeared to Haggai and had given him a message of challenge for the remnant to resume the rebuilding of the temple. And the work of building the temple was begun. Then two months before Zechariah's vision, the prophet Haggai had delivered a very sharp message to the priests because they were impure and yet were expecting God to bless them. Also, his message had been directed to the people because of their delay in building and their hesitation in moving forward with it. At this time Haggai also had told them about the coming destruction of gentile world power before God would establish His Kingdom here upon the earth. He had told them that the one who would rule would be the Messiah and that He was coming from the line of Zerubbabel, who was the civil ruler of Jerusalem at this time and was in the royal line of King David.

Now it was during this time, while the temple was being rebuilt, that Zechariah was given ten visions.

> I saw by night, and behold a man riding upon a red
> horse, and he stood among the myrtle trees that were in
> the bottom; and behind him were there red horses,
> speckled, and white [Zech. 1:8].

"I saw by night"—he doesn't say, "I dreamed by night." You may get the impression that because Zechariah had these visions at night that they were dreams, but he makes it clear that they were visions, not dreams. He was wide awake, and I don't think that any tranquilizer or sleeping pill could have put him to sleep on that night!

Many people differ with me in my stand that God does not speak through dreams or by visions in our day. I don't try to correct them when they say to me, "I saw a vision last night." I simply ask them if they saw the vision in a dream. If they did, I know immediately that God has not given them a message but that the dream was caused by something they ate for dinner the evening before, or it came out of some experience they had. In sleep the mind is unlatched or released, and it generally wanders back over some experience that produces the dream. Therefore, I think we can be sure that God does not speak to us in dreams.

Notice that Zechariah said, "I *saw*." It is important to understand how God revealed Himself to this prophet at this time.

"Behold"—Zechariah introduces his vision in a dramatic way. Frankly, I think the translator should have put an exclamation mark after that word. *Behold* means "to look." "Look! There's a man riding upon a red horse!"

"A man riding upon a red horse." Who is this man? He is the Lord Jesus Christ before His incarnation. You may ask how I know that. Well, He is identified as the "angel of the LORD" in verses 11 and 12. In the Old Testament the angel of the LORD is designated as God. Therefore, the angel of the LORD in the Old Testament is the Lord Jesus Christ of the New Testament. He is the angel of the Presence; He is Jehovah Himself, the Messiah.

Here in Christ's preincarnation Zechariah sees Him watching over this world. Now, it is true that Satan is called the prince of this world, that is, of this world system—the carnality of this world today is all under Satan's control—but God has not given up this earth to Satan. Even at this very moment, the Lord Jesus Christ is standing in the shadows, keeping watch over His own. Here in Zechariah's vision it is the nation of Israel in particular over which He is watching. What a comfort it is to know that, out of all the galaxies about us which cannot be numbered for multitude, the God of the universe is watching, keeping watch over His own. What a message this vision has for us. Zechariah will give many messages of comfort, and certainly this is one of them.

Notice that the man is riding "upon a red horse." What is the significance of the color red? Well, red speaks of blood and bloodshed; in the book of Revelation it speaks of bloodshed in war. But for this one who is riding the red horse, it speaks of His own blood that was to be shed. He is watching over this earth because He would die and shed His blood for the human family on this earth. What a picture we have here!

"Behind him were there red horses, speckled, and white." It does not say that there were riders on the horses, but I feel that we can rightly assume that each horse had a rider. Here is an instance where God has not given us complete information, but we assume that the riders are angelic beings under Christ's command whose business it is to watch over this earth and report their findings to Him. I believe that the colors of the horses—red, sorrel (called speckled in the King James Version), and white—all have significance.

I haven't seen the word sorrel since I was a boy in West Texas and Southern Oklahoma when horses were the means of transportation. I can remember when I saw my first automobile in Springer, Oklahoma. We stood and looked at it for two hours. Can you imagine going to a parking lot today and looking at a car for that long? Well, we did. A doctor owned it, and everyone in that little town in which I lived came out to look at the car. It was fearful to behold and an unusual contraption. Nobody thought it could ever supplant the horse in our day of muddy roads. I remember well the sorrel horses; they were spotted, brownish orange—I always though of them as a dirty yellow. You might not like that description if a sorrel horse is your pet, but as a boy that is the way they looked to me.

As I said, I believe there is a significance in the colors of the horses. Red horses would be symbolic of warfare. White horses would probably represent victory, symbolic of the fact that the one riding the horse is marching to victory. The sorrel is a mixture of the other colors.

"He stood among the myrtle trees." The myrtle tree is what we here in California call the laurel tree. We find it down in the desert regions. The Southern Pacific Railroad Company has planted them all along their tracks in the Palm Springs area so that the sand won't cover the tracks. In the land of Israel, which apparently is their native habitat, there were many myrtle-covered valleys. The myrtle is considered sort of a badge of Israel. You see, certain trees and plants represent the nation—the olive tree, the fig tree, the myrtle tree, the grapevine all have their significance. In Isaiah 41:19 (literal translation mine), God says, "I will put in the wilderness the cedar, the acacia, and the myrtle, and the olive, and I will set in the desert the cypress, the plane and the pine together." And in Isaiah 55:13 He says, "Instead of the thorn shall come up the cypress, and instead of the brier shall come up the myrtle: and it shall be to the Lord for a memorial for an everlasting sign which shall not be cut off." In modern Israel the tremendous planting of trees—and most of them are myrtle—could have real significance. It is interesting that myrtle branches together with palm branches were used in the ritual of constructing booths in the celebration of the Feast of Tabernacles. In fact, the name myrtle is the Hebrew hadhas, from which the name of Esther, hadhassah, is derived—so that a girl named Esther and another girl named Myrtle actually have the same name, referring to the myrtle tree.

"The myrtle trees that were in the bottom"—what does he mean by "the bottom"? It means down in a valley. The grove of myrtle trees would be in a valley where there was a water supply. The myrtle trees in the valley may be representative of Israel, for she was certainly down in a valley at this time.

Before we leave this verse, let me say that the rider on the red horse is a picture, I believe, of the Lord Jesus just waiting for the day to come when He will take over this earth. And in the meantime He is patrolling the earth, watching over it. And I assume that the riders on the other horses are created intelligences, supernatural beings, or angels, who are there with Him.

> Then said I, O my lord, what are these? And the angel that talked with me said unto me, I will shew thee what these be [Zech. 1:9].

"Then said I, O my lord, what are these?" That is the same question we have; so let's listen. He says that he will show us what these things are—

> And the man that stood among the myrtle trees answered and said, These are they whom the LORD hath sent to walk to and fro through the earth [Zech. 1:10].

"To walk to and fro" means that they were patrolling the earth.

> And they answered the angel of the LORD that stood among the myrtle trees, and said, We have walked to and fro through the earth, and, behold, all the earth sitteth still, and is at rest [Zech. 1:11].

"All the earth sitteth still, and is at rest" means that there was peace on the earth at this time. That sounds good because during five thousand years of recorded history, there have been only about two hundred years of peace. Man is a fierce, warlike creature—there is war in his heart. So a period of peace sounds wonderful. But what kind of peace was it? Well, it was the kind of peace that does not last very long.

> Then the angel of the LORD answered and said, O LORD of hosts, how long wilt thou not have mercy on Jerusalem and on the cities of Judah, against which thou hast had indignation these threescore and ten years? [Zech. 1:12].

"Against which thou hast had indignation these threescore and ten years"—that is, for seventy years now Jerusalem has been lying in ruin, debris, and ashes. But the remnant of Israel which has returned to the land is beginning to rebuild. The cry is, "How long will it be before God is going to bring real blessing to us?"

God will make it clear that He is displeased with the nations which are at peace and ignore Jerusalem's plight. God is jealous for Jerusalem, and all the nations of the world are indifferent to it. God returned to Jerusalem with mercies, and the nations have a responsibility also. But the nations are at peace, although they won't be at peace very long.

My friend, this has application to our present world situation. The world can never have permanent peace until the Lord Jesus is reigning in Jerusalem because He is the Prince of Peace. In the meantime, the peace which He offers is peace with God because of sins forgiven. If we are right with God, we can have peace with our neighbors and even peace among nations. But the so-called civilized—not Christian—nations are the ones that have carried on two world wars in this century. It is interesting that during World War II when some of our United States troops were fighting in the South Pacific, they expected to find on many of the little islands headhunters and cannibals, but instead they found Christian churches and Christians who received them joyfully. The so-called heathen were at peace, and the so-called Christians were at war! The world cannot have peace apart from Christ.

Jerusalem is the key to world peace. In Zechariah's day the world was trying to have peace and ignore Jerusalem. This was during the world domination by Media-Persia. You remember that Babylon had put down both Egypt and Assyria; then Media-Persia had put down the Babylonian Empire and was reigning all the way from the Indus River to the Mediterranean Sea and all the way from the snow of the mountains around the Black Sea and Caspian Sea to the burning sands of the Sahara Desert. Their dominion brought a brief period of peace to the world. But it wouldn't be long until Alexander the great would come out of the West and upset the apple cart again. Peace could not be permanent because the city of Jerusalem was the key to peace.

> And the LORD answered the angel that talked with me
> with good words and comfortable words [Zech. 1:13].

Notice that they were good words and comforting words, words that were helpful to the remnant. During this time Haggai was pronouncing judgment, but not Zechariah—he was giving God's message of comfort.

> So the angel that communed with me said unto me, Cry
> thou, saying, Thus saith the LORD of hosts; I am jealous
> for Jerusalem and for Zion with a great jealousy [Zech.
> 1:14].

"I am jealous for Jerusalem." God's jealousy is not a human sort of jealousy that might be just a flare of bad temper. But men's jealousy, which is a burning passion for that which is their own and is dear to them and may be taken away from them, may be similar to the jealousy of God. "I am jealous for Jerusalem and for Zion with a *great* jealousy." Jerusalem is His city, and the Israelites are His people. He is fully aware of the worldwide woe of oppressed Israel even in our day, and He is exceedingly jealous for His people. I believe that in time God is going to move on their behalf. The world then and now is ready to forsake them.

> And I am very sore displeased with the heathen that are
> at ease: for I was but a little displeased, and they helped
> forward the affliction [Zech. 1:15].

"I was but a little displeased," that is, God's chastisement was intended for a brief period, but the nations of the world wanted her annihilation.

Therefore thus saith the Lord; I am returned to Jerusalem with mercies: my house shall be built in it, saith the Lord of hosts, and a line shall be stretched forth upon Jerusalem [Zech. 1:16].

"I am returned to Jerusalem with mercies." God had come back to deal with His people in mercy. The Scriptures tell us that He is rich in mercy.

"A line shall be stretched forth upon Jerusalem." There are those who believe that this "line" stretching forth upon Jerusalem means that there would be a great building boom in Jerusalem, that it would expand and become a great city in that day. I think that is probably true. But in the Scriptures, whenever we find a man with a measuring rod or a measuring line, it means that God is getting ready to move *directly* in that particular case. In this case, Israel had just returned from the seventy-year captivity, and God is turning to His people again, turning to those who have returned to Him.

All the nations of the earth are to understand that there will never be peace on earth until there is peace in Jerusalem. That is the key to peace on this earth. Haven't we seen this demonstrated again in these last few years? Haven't the events since Israel became a nation again rather indicated that? That little nation found out how few friends she really had in the world at the beginning of the oil crisis. The nations which they thought were their friends fell away like dead flies because they wanted oil more than they wanted the friendship of Israel. But, of course, modern Israel has not returned to God in spite of the fact that there is a great building boom over there today. They have returned back to the land and have begun rebuilding the cities, and Zionism is very much a reality, yet they are actually still scattered throughout the world in disbelief. And they are still suffering persecution. The peace of Jerusalem is the key to world peace. You can see this by checking back in the history of the past.

It is certainly true that Jerusalem is crucial in the prophecies of the future: "For the Lord hath chosen Zion; he hath desired it for his habitation. This is my rest for ever: here will I dwell; for I have desired it" (Ps. 132:13–14). Also, "Moreover he refused the tabernacle of Joseph, and chose not the tribe of Ephraim: but chose the tribe of Judah, the mount Zion which he loved" (Ps. 78:67-68). God says that Jerusalem is the spot He loves. I must confess that I do not love Jerusalem as it is today. I must be very frank to say that it is not an attractive place to me. But God is going to make it a wonderful place some day. Although the judgment of God is upon Jerusalem even in this day, God still loves it.

> Cry yet, saying, Thus saith the LORD of hosts; My cities through prosperity shall yet be spread abroad; and the LORD shall yet comfort Zion, and shall yet choose Jerusalem [Zech. 1:17].

This looks into the future so that these people can recognize that they are working in the plan and program of God which extends into the future.

Allow me to make an application for Christians today. Are you and I working in something that has eternal value? What are you doing today? What value will it be ten years from today? A hundred years from today? A million years from today? Are you and I actually working in the light of eternity? We should keep that in mind.

VISION OF FOUR HORNS

This is the second vision given to Zechariah.

> Then lifted I up mine eyes, and saw, and behold four horns.
>
> And I said unto the angel that talked with me, What be these? And he answered me, These are the horns which have scattered Judah, Israel, and Jerusalem [Zech. 1:18-19].

I consider the vision of the four horns as one vision, and the vision of the four carpenters as another vision. Most expositors combine them and consider them as a single vision, but I do not interpret them that way.

Zechariah sees four horns, and these four horns are the ones that scattered Jerusalem and Judah and Israel. They scattered both the northern and the southern kingdoms.

A horn represents a gentile ruler. We find this in Daniel 7:24: "And the ten horns out of this kingdom are ten kings that shall arise . . . ." Again, in Revelation 17:12: "And the ten horns which thou sawest are ten kings, which have received no kingdom as yet; but receive power as kings one hour with the beast." I think you can see from these other references that horns represent gentile world powers. So these four horns which Zechariah saw represent four gentile world powers.

Well, who are they? The four gentile powers that scattered Israel are: Babylon, Media-Persia, Greece, and Rome. The interesting thing is that in the next vision God makes it very clear that these four horns will be dealt with.

THE VISION OF FOUR SMITHS

In our text they are called carpenters, but they are actually skilled workmen or artisans—or they can be called smiths because a smith is a trained workman.

> And the LORD shewed me four carpenters.
>
> Then said I, What come these to do? And he spake, saying, These are the horns which have scattered Judah, so that no man did lift up his head: but these are come to fray them, to cast out the horns of the Gentiles, which lifted up their horn over the land of Judah to scatter it [Zech. 1:20–21].

"Then said I, What come these to do?" That is, "What are these skilled workmen doing here?"

"And he spake, saying, These are the horns which have scattered Judah, so that no man did lift up his head: but these are come to fray [terrify] them, to cast out the horns of the Gentiles [nations], which lifted up their horn over the land of Judah to scatter it." This is, without doubt, one of the most remarkable prophecies we have in the Scriptures.

Who are the four smiths? There have been many suggestions. Jerome and Cyril and Calvin considered them symbolic of the supernatural means which God uses. Well, I don't quite agree with that. The smiths or artisans are workmen which build up something. I am greatly indebted to Dr. Merrill Unger for his interpretation, which I consider to be the correct one. (By the way, Dr. Unger's book on Zechariah is the finest I have seen.) Since the four horns are symbolic of four successive world empires spanning ". . . the times of the Gentiles . . ." (Luke 21:24), the four smiths must also represent four successive powers used by God to terrify and to cast down the enemies of God's people Israel. Now let me quote Dr. Unger from *Unger's Bible Commentary: Zechariah* (p. 40):

> In line with Daniel's great prophecies concerning "the times of the Gentiles" (Dan. 2:31–45; 7:2–13) three of the **horns** in turn and under the punitive hand of God *become* **smiths**, while the fourth and last horn is cast down by the world–wide kingdom set up by the returning Christ, coming to dash to pieces His enemies who are at the same time His peoples' enemies (Ps. 2:1–12). Thus the first horn (Babylon) is cast down by Medo–Persia, the second horn. The second horn (Medo–Persia), accordingly, in turn becomes the first smith. The second horn (Medo–Persia) is cast down by the third horn, and thus becomes the second smith. The third horn (Macedonian Greece), is in turn cast down by the fourth horn (Rome), which thus becomes the third smith. The fourth horn (Rome), the most dreadful of all, *does not* become a smith but in its revived ten–kingdom form of the last days is destroyed by the fourth smith, *the millennial Kingdom* set up by the returning "King of kings and Lord of lords" (Rev. 19:16).

The interesting thing is that if you study the history of Rome, you will see that Rome was not destroyed by an outside power. In fact, according to prophecy, the Roman Empire will come back together again. It never did die—it just fell apart because of the internal corruption of the kingdom. There is one who is coming, the Antichrist, who will restore the Roman Empire. He will be a world dictator. Who is going to put him down? Christ will put him down when He returns to the earth. Therefore, Christ is represented by the fourth carpenter or smith. He is the One who will put down the Roman Empire when He comes at the end of the Great Tribulation period.

My friend, I hope this enables you to see how important it is to study the entire Word of God, because ". . . no prophecy of the scripture is of any private interpretation . . ." (2 Pet. 1:20)—that is, it is not to be interpreted by itself. It must be fitted into God's tremendous program that reaches on into eternity.

It is interesting that, when the Lord Jesus came to earth the first time, He had the title of the Carpenter of Nazareth. And He is coming again someday as a carpenter to put down this world dictator and establish His Kingdom here upon this earth with Jerusalem as its center. Someone has expressed it in these words:

> Then let the world forbear their rage,
> The Church renounce her fear;
> Israel must live through every age,
> And be the Almighty's care.
> —Author unknown

Before we leave this chapter, I would like to call your attention to the fact that great prominence is given in each of the ten visions to these truths: (1) that God is not through with the nation Israel; and (2) when God says Israel and Judah and Jerusalem, He means exactly those geographic locations. The modern cult which teaches that Great Britain and the United States are the "ten lost tribes" is entirely wrong. I suppose that it helps our national pride to believe that we might be the "chosen people." However, the only way God chooses people today is in Christ. It makes no difference who you are, what your color is, or what your station in life happens to be, if you are in

Christ, you are chosen and accepted in the Beloved. Unless we are in Christ, it makes no difference to what nation we belong—right now it wouldn't be helpful even to belong to the nation of Israel. We are looking for a ". . . city . . .whose builder and maker is God" (Heb. 11:10), and it is coming from God out of heaven someday. That is our hope.

But God is going to make good His promises to Israel. He will be faithful to them. If you could persuade me that He is going to be unfaithful to the nation Israel, then I do not know on what basis I could believe that He is going to be faithful to the church. But God *is* faithful, both to us and to Israel.

CHAPTER 2

THEME: *Vision of the man with the measuring line*

The vision of this chapter prophesies the rebuilding of the temple and the city of Jerusalem by the remnant of Israel in the days of Zechariah. However, this in no way concludes the prophecy. Zechariah—and this is true of all the other prophets—looks forward to the very end times and sees the rebuilding of Jerusalem and the temple during the Millennium. During this period the desert will blossom as the rose—and there is a whole lot of desert to blossom over there! And the Lord Himself will dwell in the city of Jerusalem. Although I don't like Jerusalem as it is today, when the Lord moves into it, I think both you and I will like it then. (However, we won't be living there because the New Jerusalem will be the home of the church.) But the earthly Jerusalem will be inhabited and will become the center of this earth. Keep in mind that the Lord will do this—He has already said in chapter 1 verse 17, "My cities through prosperity shall yet be spread abroad; and the LORD shall yet comfort Zion, and shall yet choose Jerusalem." So you see, everything that was to be done in Zechariah's day had eternal significance. God has a purpose with Israel—He is not about to cast her off. Although local circumstances in Zechariah's day were discouraging and it seemed that God has deserted them, He wanted them to know that not only had He not deserted them, but He has an eternal plan and purpose for them. They could say with us, "Being confident of this very thing, that he which hath begun a good work in you will perform it until the day of Jesus Christ" (Phil. 1:6).

VISION OF THE MAN WITH THE MEASURING LINE

> I lifted up mine eyes again, and looked, and behold a
> man with a measuring line in his hand [Zech. 2:1].

"I lifted up mine eyes again, and looked." Zechariah sees it with his physical eyes; he is not asleep.

"Behold a man with a measuring line." The appearance of this man reveals that He is the angel of the Lord, the preincarnate Christ, the same one who appeared in the first vision as the rider on the red horse. You may wonder why I say that He is the angel of the Lord when Zechariah simply calls him a man. Well, Zechariah presents Him as a man (ish in Hebrew). In Chapter 6 verse 12 Zechariah will say, "Thus speaketh the LORD of hosts, saying, Behold the man whose name is The BRANCH." That is the branch of David, the sprout which is coming from Jesse, the Lord Jesus Christ.

To determine the meaning of the "measuring line," I want to call your attention to other verses of Scripture: "Behold, the days come, saith the LORD, that the city shall be built to the LORD from the tower of Hananeel unto the gate of the corner. And the measuring line shall yet go forth over against it upon the hill Gareb, and shall compass about to Goath" (Jer. 31:38–39). When you find God using a measuring line, it simply means that He is getting ready to move again in behalf of that which He is measuring. In the Jeremiah reference He is measuring the city of Jerusalem. The prophet Ezekiel also speaks of measuring. "In the visions of God brought he me into the land of Israel, and set me upon a very high mountain, by which was as the frame of a city on the south. And he brought me thither, and, behold, there was a man, whose appearance was like the appearance of brass, with a line of flax in his hand, and a measuring reed; and he stood in the gate. And the man said unto me, Son of man, behold with thine eyes, and hear with thine ears, and set thine heart upon all that I shall shew thee; for to the intent that I might shew them unto thee art thou brought hither: declare all that thou seest to the house of Israel" (Ezek. 40:2–4). If we read further we would see that this is the vision of the building of the millennial temple in Jerusalem. There is another reference concerning a measuring line: "And there was given me a reed like unto a rod: and the angel stood, saying, Rise, and measure the temple of God, and the altar, and them that worship therein. But the court which is without the temple leave out, and measure it not; for it is given unto the Gentiles: and the holy city shall they tread under foot forty and two months" (Rev. 11:1–2). Without going into detail, let me say that this again is the measuring of the millennial temple that is to be built.

> Then said I, Whither goest thou? And he said unto me,
> To measure Jerusalem, to see what is the breadth
> thereof, and what is the length thereof [Zech. 2:2].

"Whither goest thou?" Zechariah is interested and asks, "Where in the world are you going with that measuring line?"

"To measure Jerusalem, to see what is the breadth . . . and what is the length." He is saying that the city is to be expanded. It did that in Zechariah's day, and it is certainly doing that now. It spilled over the walls long ago. On every hill around the old city of Jerusalem there is construction going on. I don't consider the current building program to be a fulfillment of Zechariah's prophecy because I believe the fulfillment is yet future. The Jews could be driven out of the land of Israel again without disturbing God's promise to eventually and finally bring them back to the land—for that is exactly what He intends to do.

> And, behold, the angel that talked with me went forth,
> and another angel went out to meet him,
>
> And said unto him, Run, speak to this young man, say-
> ing, Jerusalem shall be inhabited as towns without
> walls for the multitude of men and cattle therein [Zech.
> 2:3-4].

"Run, speak to this young man." The young man is evidently Zechariah.

"Jerusalem shall be inhabited as towns without walls." In our day the walls of Jerusalem surround only the older city, the small Arab city. Most of the city is outside the walls, scattered on the surrounding hills. This will also be true when this prophecy is fulfilled in the future. It won't be needful to have walls because (1) in modern warfare walls afford no protection, and (2) the city will be at peace, which means that the Prince of Peace will be reigning in Jerusalem.

> For I, saith the LORD, will be unto her a wall of fire round
> about, and will be the glory in the midst of her [Zech.
> 2:5].

This certainly is not true in our day. Their help comes from other nations. But God says that in the future He will be a wall of fire around them. This means that *God* will be their protection. And, my friend, when God protects them, that will be miraculous. Not only will He be their protection, but He Himself will be in their midst. In other words, the *shekinah* glory will then be back in the temple—it did not return to the little temple which the remnant built in the days of Zechariah. But to the harassed little remnant God is promising His protection, He is saying essentially the same thing which he said to Abraham after he had delivered Lot: ". . . Fear not, Abram: I am thy shield, and thy exceeding great reward" (Gen. 15:1). This means that God will make good all that He had promised them.

Daniel, Ezekiel, Zechariah, and Revelation are the four apocalyptic books in the Bible. They all look to the future when the Kingdom is to be established here upon earth. I would like to quote a rather extensive passage from Ezekiel 43 to show the glory that is coming. It describes the coming of the Lord Jesus, the Messiah, into His temple. "Afterward he brought me to the gate, even the gate that looketh toward the east: And, behold, the glory of the God of Israel came from the way of the east: and his voice was like a noise of many waters: and the earth shined with his glory."

This is the Lord Jesus, the Messiah, coming into the temple. Notice that He is coming from the east, which is the reason the Eastern Gate in the wall of Jerusalem is so prominent even in our day, although it is sealed up. Facing that gate are graves of thousands of Israelites because they believe they will be resurrected when this prophecy is fulfilled—and they want to be present when the Messiah comes. "And it was according to the appearance of the vision which I saw, even according to the vision that I saw when I came to destroy the city: and the visions were like the vision that I saw by the river Chebar; and I fell upon my face. And the glory of the LORD came into the house by the way of the gate whose prospect is toward the east. So the spirit took me up, and brought me into the inner court; and, behold, the glory of the LORD filled the house. And I heard him speaking unto me out of the house; and the man stood by me. And he said unto me, Son of man, the place of my throne, and the place of the soles of my feet, where I will dwell in the midst of the children of Israel for ever, and my holy name, shall the house of Israel no more defile, neither they, nor their kings, by their whoredom, nor by the carcases of their kings in their high places" (Ezek. 43:3-7).

Notice it says, "I will dwell in the midst of the children of Israel for ever." Forever is a long time, my friend, You see, this is a prophecy that does not find its fulfillment in the days of Ezekiel but looks down through the ages to the Millennium, the time when the Lord Jesus will come and establish His Kingdom here on earth.

Now note again what Zechariah has prophesied: "For I, saith the Lord, will be unto her a wall of fire round about, and will be the glory in the midst of her."

> Ho, ho, come forth, and flee from the land of the north,
> saith the Lord: for I have spread you abroad as the four
> winds of the heaven, saith the Lord [Zech. 2:6].

"Ho, ho" is a call to listen. One "ho" would be enough, but when there is a double "ho," it means that He is giving them something very important, and in this case it is a warning.

"Come forth, and flee from the land of the north." In the following verse we shall see that Babylon is referred to as "the land of the north," although it is actually situated in an easterly direction from Palestine. It is called the land of the north because invading armies and trading caravans from that land to Jerusalem came around the route called the "fertile crescent" and entered Palestine from the north.

"I have spread you abroad as the four winds of the heaven, saith the Lord." Although historical Babylon did fall two years after this prophecy was given, the final fulfillment will be in the last days when God will regather them from their worldwide dispersion.

> Deliver thyself, O Zion, that dwellest with the daughter
> of Babylon [Zech. 2:7].

This means to get out of Babylon. Why? Because Babylon was going to fall. God was going to bring it down. Let me revert to the two visions about the horns and the carpenters. The first horn is Babylon, and now the carpenter (representing Medo-Persia) is coming, and he is going to tear Babylon down. But Medo-Persia will become a great power, a horn, and then he will persecute God's people. So God will move that nation off the scene by bringing in another carpenter, which will be Greece. And Greece will become a proud nation. And under a ruler, Antiochus Epiphanes, who will come out of the divided empire of Alexander the Great, Israel will be severely persecuted. Then God will raise up another carpenter, Rome, and he will cut down the power of Greece. When the Roman Empire becomes a great power, where is the carpenter who will cut it down? History tells us that the great Roman Empire fell apart, but prophecy tells us that it will come back together again in the last days. Then who will put it down? The Lord Jesus is going to come from heaven. He is the Carpenter of Nazareth, and He is also the man with the measuring rod. He will put down the Antichrist and his kingdom. Then Christ will establish His own Kingdom here upon the earth. This is the picture given to us in these visions, which makes them of utmost significance.

> For thus saith the LORD of hosts; After the glory hath he
> sent me unto the nations which spoiled you: for he that
> toucheth you toucheth the apple of his eye [Zech. 2:8].

"Apple of his eye" is an unusual expression, although it occurs elsewhere in Scripture. In this instance it is the Hebrew *babah*, meaning "the pupil" or "the gate" (through which light enters). It is an expression which indicates that which is most precious, most easily injured, and most demanding of protection. This is what Israel is to the Lord God.

> For, behold, I will shake mine hand upon them, and
> they shall be a spoil to their servants: and ye shall know
> that the LORD of hosts hath sent me [Zech. 2:9].

"I will shake mine hand upon them"—that is, all God needs to do is to shake His hand threatening against the enemies of His people. "And they shall be a spoil to their servants." Those who served them shall become their masters.

Now here is one of the great prophecies of Scripture.

> **Sing and rejoice, O daughter of Zion: for, lo, I come, and I will dwell in the midst of thee, saith the LORD [Zech. 2:10].**

"Sing and rejoice, O daughter of Zion." Zion is a hill over in Jerusalem. There are cults that want to appropriate this verse to themselves; so they have moved "Zion" to England or to the United States. Let's be clear on this: When God speaks of Zion, He is not talking about Illinois or Utah or any place other than Palestine. There is a constant danger of taking these prophecies which were given to Israel and relating them to us by way of *interpretation.* Certainly we can make *application* to our own country and to our own lives because great principles are stated here. But when God is talking about geography, He means exactly what He says. "But," somebody says, "this is a vision." Granted, but a vision is a vision of reality. A friend of mine disagreed with my interpretation of the Book of Revelation. He said, "It doesn't mean that."

I said, "Then you tell me what it means."

"It is a symbol."

"All right, now you tell me what it is a symbol *of.*"

"Oh, it's just a symbol."

"Don't you know that a symbol has to be a symbol *of* something? And it has to make sense. You can't just pull an explanation out of a hat and say, 'This is what it means.' How do you know what it means? It is a symbol of something, and by careful study and comparison with parallel passages, you are to determine what it is. No prophecy is of 'private interpretation'; it must be tested by the whole Word of God."

Therefore, when God uses a geographical term like Zion, He is talking about Zion in Israel. And notice that He is addressing the "daughter of Zion," which is the nation Israel. This is a very familiar figure for Israel, and it cannot mean any other people.

"Lo, I come, and I will dwell in the midst of thee, saith the LORD."

God means this literally. He intends to come to that geographical spot on the earth called Zion and to a certain group of people who will be there, Israel the daughter of Zion.

> And many nations shall be joined to the LORD in that day, and shall be my people: and I will dwell in the midst of thee, and thou shalt know that the LORD of hosts hath sent me unto thee.

> And the LORD shall inherit Judah his portion in the holy land, and shall choose Jerusalem again [Zech. 2:11–12].

"And many nations shall be joined to the LORD in that day." Notice that it is not only Israel, but *many* nations will be converted to Christ in that day. To be "joined to the LORD" is to be united to Him in faith and spiritual experience.

"And the LORD shall inherit Judah." The conversion of "many nations" does not imply that God will not fulfill His promises to Judah. Zechariah reminds his people again that they are God's inheritance and His portion.

This ought to answer once and for all the anti-Semite who insists that *Judah* refers to Jews and that *Israel* refers to another race. God says that He intends to inherit *Judah*.

"His portion in the holy land." This is the only place in the Bible where the phrase "holy land" is used. It is not the *holy* land today. When I make this statement publicly, it is generally challenged by somebody who says, "But it *is* the holy land. That is the place where Jesus walked!" Well, His footprints are all gone. He is not walking there now. However, someday He will return, and when He does, it will be the holy land again.

"And shall choose Jerusalem again" implies that He is not choosing Jerusalem right now—and I wouldn't either! But when He does choose it, it will become the capital of this earth.

Remember that no prophecy is of any "private interpretation." It must parallel other Scriptures. So let me call your attention to a parallel passage in Isaiah: "And it shall come to pass in the last days, that the mountain of the LORD's house shall be established in the top of the mountains, and shall be exalted above the hills; and all nations shall flow unto it. And many people shall go and say, Come ye, and let us go up to the mountain of the LORD, to the house of the God of Jacob; and he will teach us of his ways, and we will walk in his paths: for out of Zion shall go forth the law, and the word of the LORD from Jerusalem" (Isa. 2:2–3). All of this looks forward to the time of the Millennium.

> **Be silent, O all flesh, before the LORD: for he is raised up out of his holy habitation [Zech. 2:13].**

In that day the whole earth will keep silence. Today we hear a lot about freedom of speech, but in that future day there is going to be a marvelous freedom of silence. Why? Because God will be in His holy temple. This looks forward to His visible presence on earth during the Millennium.

This prospect for the future should have been an encouragement to those people in the day of Zechariah. I'm sure it was. And it ought to be an encouragement for us today. God has a plan and purpose for each one of us. He is working in your life and in my life. He works in our hearts both to will and to do of His good pleasure. Oh, to be in step with Him and to be going in the same direction as He is going!

CHAPTER 3

As we continue in our study of the ten visions which God gave to
Zechariah, keep in mind that we are in a highly figurative section of the Word of God. These ten visions should be considered together as focusing on one particular message. An overall viewpoint
will give us a perspective of what each vision is trying to tell us. Also,
we need to compare them with other prophetic Scripture passages. As
the apostle Peter said, ". . . no prophecy of the scripture is of any
private interpretation" (2 Pet. 1:20). That is, we are not to interpret it
by itself, but compare it with the whole program of prophecy to get the
overall viewpoint which reaches from eternity past to eternity future.

VISION OF JOSHUA AND SATAN

> And he shewed me Joshua the high priest standing be-
> fore the angel of the Lord, and Satan standing at his
> right hand to resist him [Zech. 3:1].

"He shewed me Joshua the high priest." Keep in mind that this is not
the Joshua who led the children of Israel into the Promised Land. This
is the Joshua who served as high priest among the remnant of Israel
who returned to Jerusalem after the Babylonian captivity. The name
Joshua means "Jehovah saves," and in the Greek language of the New
Testament, the name is translated as "Jesus." You remember that the
angel in announcing His approaching birth said, ". . . thou shalt call
his name JESUS: for he shall save his people from their sins" (Matt.
1:21). So you can see that the name *Joshua* is especially appropriate
for this high priest and prefigures what the nation Israel ought to have
been—that is, a holy, high-priestly nation.

"Standing before the angel of the Lord." This angel is the Lord

Jesus Christ before His incarnation, as we have seen in the previous chapters.

"And Satan standing at his right hand." It is quite obvious that if Zechariah *saw* Joshua, he also *saw* Satan, which means that Satan is a reality and a person.

In our contemporary culture we see a revival in interest regarding Satan. He pretty much had dropped out of the vocabulary of most people in so-called Christian lands for the past fifty years. They had forgotten about him; or perhaps they felt that by not mentioning him he would go away. But he hasn't gone away. He is very much a reality. The current interest in the supernatural has turned, unfortunately, to Satan and to demons rather than to God and the Lord Jesus Christ. The Bible tells us, and modern thinking demands, that evil be incarnate, that it be represented by a person. Therefore, many folk have gone off into demonology. Logically, if evil must be personified, then good must also be personified. Good is God, and God is good. God in the person of the Lord Jesus Christ will be the final answer to men who are seeking a solution to their own problems and to the ills of the world.

"To resist him." The fact that Satan is standing at Joshua's right hand could mean that he is there to support him or defend him, but, no, he is there to bring charges against him. This is typical in the workings of Satan. Scripture tells us that you and I have an advocate with God the Father. Why do we need an advocate with God the Father? Because of the enemy who is accusing us. In Revelation 12:10 he is called ". . . the accuser of our brethren . . .which accused them before our God day and night." I have a notion that this very day he has made a charge against McGee, and I'm sure it is a valid charge. And I am confident that he has been making charges against me from the time I became a child of God. When I was in my teens, working in a Nashville bank, I had tried every form of sin imaginable at that time and was one of a very fast crowd. I was the last person in that crowd that anybody would have imagined would ever go into the ministry and become a teacher of the Word of God. After God had saved me and when I felt God was calling me into the ministry, I made that announcement at the bank and resigned from my position. I wish you could have heard the guffaws that went out. "Imagine McGee!" And I suppose that Satan had a busy day accusing me before the Lord—"You would be very foolish to let him into the ministry. That fellow is the last person in this entire area who ought to go into the ministry." And Satan was standing at the right hand of Joshua to resist him, to accuse him. He was probably saying to God, "How can you put up with this man—he is filthy!" Also Satan was the accuser of the nation Israel. He is really an anti-Semite. If you want to know who is the leader of anti-Semitism, it is the Devil himself.

However, as God's children we have an advocate with the Father. John, writing to believers, says, "My little children, these things write I unto you, that ye sin not. [I wish we didn't, but we do.] And if any man sin, we have an advocate with the Father, Jesus Christ the righteous" (1 John 2:1). And Jesus Christ is the "angel of the LORD" before whom Joshua the high priest is standing in this vision of Zechariah.

> **And the LORD said unto Satan, The LORD rebuke thee, O Satan; even the LORD that hath chosen Jerusalem rebuke thee: is not this a brand plucked out of the fire? [Zech. 3:2].**

"The LORD rebuke thee" is very gentle, according to my standards. I could think of a stronger rebuke than that, but God respects this one whom He created. Remember that God created him ". . . Lucifer, son of the morning . . ." (Isa. 14:12), probably the highest creature that He ever created. Then sin was found in him. What kind of sin? Lust or stealing? No. Pride was found in him. He had a free will and set that will against the will of God. My friend, that is sin. "All we like sheep have gone astray; we have turned every one to his own way . . ." (Isa. 53:6). Specific sins such as murder, stealing, lying, adultery all come under the heading of "his own way." This is the problem of mankind.

"Even the LORD that hath chosen Jerusalem rebuke thee." This reveals that the rebuke comes not on the account of Joshua the person but on account of Jerusalem, the capital of the nation.

"Is not this a brand plucked out of the fire?" It looked as if Jerusalem could never be rebuilt after Nebuchadnezzar destroyed it, and it lay in dust and ashes for seventy years. Then out of the ruins the city is rebuilt—a brand plucked out of the burning.

John Wesley called himself a brand plucked out of the burning. I'm of the opinion that many of us today think of ourselves in that way. As I look back, it seems like an accident that I got saved. It just didn't seem that it could possibly have happened to me. But it did happen, and I know now that it was no accident at all. It can be said of any sinner who comes to Christ that he is a brand plucked out of the fire.

> **Now Joshua was clothed with filthy garments, and stood before the angel [Zech. 3:3].**

This vision of Joshua the high priest actually goes beyond the man himself. We will learn that this vision gives us the answer to a very difficult question. This is the problem: We have learned so far that God is going to return the nation Israel to the land and that He will dwell in the midst of them. They will be totally restored as His people. That hasn't happened yet, but He says He is going to do that. He will bless them in that land. How can God do that when the people are far from Him? In the day of Zechariah they were far from God and living in sin. Today the same thing is true. How can it ever be a holy land when sinners are living in it?

Unger states the problem in this way:

> In the preceding visions the marvellous purposes of God's grace toward Israel appear in the judgment of her enemies and the restoration of both the land and of the people. But a crucial question arises: How can an infinitely holy God accomplish such plans with a sinful and besmirched people? How can the wondrous manifestations of divine mercy to them be consistent with God's righteousness? (*Unger's Bible Commentary: Zechariah*, p. 55).

I think the explanation to this problem will become clear as we study the vision. Joshua was to represent the nation. As we read on, we will find him clothed with a filthy garment, very dirty. If you will remember our study of the high priest, you will recall that the high priest had to be dressed spotlessly or else he was not permitted to serve God. Joshua really was the high priest at this time, but in this vision he also represented the entire nation.

Joshua as an individual was not a perfect individual. Even though he was God's high priest, he was described as dirty and filthy. That might have been true of him personally, I do not know. But I do know that the high priest has always represented the nation Israel. For example, on the great Day of Atonement, the high priest went into the Holy of Holies for the entire nation. In just the same way, Jesus Christ is our high priest. He is the representative for the corporate body of believers, the church. He appears before God for us today. To see Joshua in the context of all the ten visions of Zechariah and as a prophetic picture of the nation Israel will deliver us from a very limited interpretation.

Leupold says of the high priest:

He represents and practically impersonates Israel in his holy office. For the nation he prays; for it he enters the Holy Place, he bears the nation's guilt. We must, therefore, not refer the issues and implications of this chapter to Joshua as an individual, nor merely to Joshua, the high priest. We must conclude that his condition is Israel's condition, his acquittal a typical way of expressing theirs; the words of comfort and assurance given him apply with equal validity to them (Exposition of Zechariah, p. 64).

That is a very fine statement. Leupold is not always one we can follow in his interpretations, but in this instance he is especially good.

Joshua was a symbol, a type, a representative. God had chosen him, and God had also chosen the nation Israel.

The high priest was to be clothed in fine-twined, white linen undergarments. And over them were to be placed the garments of beauty and glory. Joshua was pictured here as the high priest representing the nation, and his garments, which should have been clean, were unclean. In fact, he "was clothed with filthy garments." That word *filthy* means that there was human excrement on them! Not only was he dirty looking, but he smelled bad. My friend, that is the way the sins of the nation Israel looked to almighty God. How can this be remedied?

A man with a question called me by telephone from Indianapolis. His question was an old one which has been asked over and over by many people down through the years. It was this: "Have I committed the unpardonable sin?" I told him, "Of course you haven't. Jesus died for *all* your sins. Regardless of who you are or what you have done, you can come to Him right now, confessing your sins and trusting Christ as your Savior. If you do that and mean it, He will forgive you. 'For Christ is the end of the law for righteousness to everyone that believeth' (Rom. 10:4). So it doesn't make any difference what you have done, you can come to God through Jesus Christ."

> And he answered and spake unto those that stood before
> him, saying, Take away the filthy garments from him.
> And unto him he said, Behold, I have caused thine iniq-
> uity to pass from thee, and I will clothe thee with
> change of raiment [Zech. 3:4].

This is, without doubt, one of the most beautiful pictures we have in the Old Testament. Joshua could not stand before a righteous, holy God with these dirty garments on. Also his weakness was revealed. You see, being dirty and filthy as he was gave Satan an advantage because the adversary could point his finger at him. Let me give you Dr. Unger's translation of verse 4: "And he answered and spake unto those that stood before him, saying, Take the filthy garments from off him. And unto him he said, Behold, I have caused thine iniquity to pass from thee, and I will clothe thee with rich apparel" (*Unger's Bible Commentary: Zechariah*, p. 60).

Joshua represented not only the nation of Israel, he represents us today. In him we see the sin of the believer. Joshua was a priest before God—God appointed priests in the Old Testament. In our day every believer is a priest before God, but some of us are standing in dirty garments. "Yes," you may say, "but I have been clothed in the righteousness of Christ." If you have been saved, that is true. And that is exactly the picture which is given to us here. You see, the dirty garments, representing sin, must be removed from him, and he must be clothed with clean garments, symbolic of the righteousness of Christ. This pictures your salvation and mine, which makes this such a precious passage of Scripture. Let me refer you to the Epistle to the Romans. In the first three chapters mankind is set before us as a sinner before God. We all stand dirty before Him. And our righteousness—even the best that we can do—is filthy rags in God's sight. We stand in Joshua's condition. What are we going to do about our plight?

Here is God's answer: "But now the righteousness of God without the law is manifested, being witnessed by the law and the prophets; even the righteousness of God which is by faith of Jesus Christ unto all and upon all them that believe: for there is no difference: for all have sinned, and come short of the glory of God; being justified freely [without cause] by his grace through the redemption that is in Christ Jesus" (Rom. 3:21–24). Why? Because Christ died, shed His blood, that it might be possible for you and me to come in our filthy rags to Him. He will not accept the filthy rags of our own righteousness. He will take them off and clothe us in the righteousness of Christ. When we stand clothed in Christ's righteousness, nobody, no created thing, can bring any charge against us because we are God's elect. Notice what Paul writes in Romans 8: "What shall we then say to these things? If God be for us, who can be against us? He that spared not his own Son, but delivered him up for us all, how shall he not with him also freely [without a cause] give us all things? Who shall lay any thing to the charge of God's elect? It is God that justifieth. Who is he that condemneth? It is Christ that died, yea rather, that is risen again, who is even at the right hand of God, who also maketh intercession for us" (Rom. 8:31–34). What a Savior we have! When we trust Him as our Savior, He not only takes from us our sins, removes the dirty garment, but He puts on us the robe of His righteousness, and no one can bring any charge against God's elect.

But wait—can God's child get into sin? Yes. Then what is the child of God to do? Well, "If we confess our sins, he is faithful and just to

forgive us our sins, and to cleanse us from all unrighteousness"
(1 John 1:9). When you and I are out of fellowship with God, we have
lost a great deal. We have lost all joy from our lives. We have lost all
power from our lives. And it is possible to lose our assurance. I am of
the opinion that many folk lack the assurance of their salvation because of sin in their lives. Another thing we lose is our privilege of
being of service to God.

You see, if Joshua is to stand before God as His high priest, he must
be wearing clean garments. And *God* provides clean garments. How?
By mercy. There was a mercy seat in the temple. And we today have a
mercy seat—"And he [Christ] is the propitiation [the mercy seat] for
our sins . . ." (1 John 2:2). How wonderful this is, and what a glorious
picture it gives of God's provision!

Now, you may have an objection to God's choosing the nation Israel. Did He choose them because they were attractive? No. He didn't
choose *me* for that reason either. I think of Ruth when she asked Boaz,
". . . Why have I found grace in thine eyes . . . ? (Ruth 2:10). Well, I
could say to her, "All you have to do is go home and look in the mirror
and you will find out why he fell in love with you and why he extended grace to you. You are beautiful. You are lovely." But, my friend,
don't tell *me* to look in the mirror. I have already done it, and what did
I see? A sinner, a sinner who needs to be clothed with the righteousness of Christ.

> **And I said, Let them set a fair mitre upon his head. So
> they set a fair mitre upon his head, and clothed him
> with garments. And the angel of the LORD stood by
> [Zech. 3:5].**

The adding of this mitre or turban is a little something which is beautiful in its symbolism. The garments of the high priest included a turban, and on that turban were the words: HOLINESS UNTO THE
LORD, as in chapter 14 verse 20. This man Joshua didn't have a turban
because in those dirty old garments he certainly was not holy to the
Lord. But a turban is given to him now on which is inscribed "Holiness unto the Lord." He will be used of God now just as Israel will be

used of the Lord in the future. After the church has been removed in the Rapture, Israel will be the witness for God during the Tribulation, and then during the Millennium the entire nation will be a priesthood down here upon this earth.

> And the angel of the LORD protested unto Joshua, saying,

> Thus saith the LORD of hosts; If thou wilt walk in my ways, and if thou wilt keep my charge, then thou shalt also judge my house, and shalt also keep my courts, and I will give thee places to walk among these that stand by [Zech. 3:6–7].

The interpretation of this is quite obvious. Joshua had been dirty, but God had a redemption which enabled Him to extend His grace and mercy to him. Now Joshua is saved, but God says, "If you want to be used, you will have to stay clean. You will have to walk in My ways. You will have to be obedient to Me."

Not only is God saying this to Joshua, He is saying it to the nation, and He is saying it to you and me today. Jesus said, "If ye love me, keep my commandments" (John 14:15). Some folk seem to have the idea that if they are saved by grace, they can do as they please. My friend, that is inconsistent. If you do as you please, you are not saved by grace—because certainly you are going to love the One who died to save you. If you have really accepted Him and are really trusting Him, you are resting upon Him. And if you are resting in Him, you will want to be obedient to Him and do as He wants you to do. It can't be any other way.

VISION OF THE BRANCH

> Hear now, O Joshua the high priest, thou, and thy fellows that sit before thee: for they are men wondered at: for, behold, I will bring forth my servant the BRANCH [Zech. 3:8].

"My servant the BRANCH" is a marvelous picture of the Lord Jesus Christ. "The Branch" is a familiar figure of the Messiah. Isaiah used that figure to predict His first coming as Savior: "And there shall come forth a rod out of the stem of Jesse, and a Branch shall grow out of his roots" (Isa. 11:1). And Jeremiah used it to speak of Christ's coming as King to this earth: "Behold, the days come, saith the LORD, that I will raise unto David a righteous Branch, and a King shall reign and prosper, and shall execute judgment and justice in the earth" (Jer. 23:5).

"Hear now, O Joshua the high priest, thou, and thy fellows that sit before thee." God is here addressing Joshua and his fellow priests. Now what is the message He is giving them? Leupold's paraphrase of verse 8 provides the answer: "I shall not let you, Joshua, and your fellow priests be removed from office, nor your office be discontinued, for I have a destiny for you—you are a type of the coming Messiah, who will do My work perfectly ('Servant'), and who will bring the priestly office to undreamed of glory ('Shoot') when He springs forth" (op. cit., in loc.).

> **For behold the stone that I have laid before Joshua; upon one stone shall be seven eyes: behold, I will engrave the graving thereof, saith the LORD of hosts, and I will remove the iniquity of that land in one day [Zech. 3:9].**

The "Branch" is also the stone, the stone which Daniel saw in the vision of the great image: "Thou sawest till that a stone was cut out without hands, which smote the image upon his feet that were of iron and clay, and brake them to pieces. Then was the iron, the clay, the brass, the silver, and the gold, broken to pieces together, and became like the chaff of the summer threshingfloors; and the wind carried them away, that no place was found for them: and the stone that smote the image became a great mountain, and filled the whole earth" (Dan. 2:34–35).

"Upon one stone shall be seven eyes." Seven is not the number of perfection but the number of completeness. The "seven eyes" indicate that Christ has complete knowledge and wisdom. In the New Testament it is said of Christ, "In whom are hid all the treasures of wisdom and knowledge" (Col. 2:3). And the Lord Jesus has been made unto us wisdom because He is all wisdom (see 1 Cor. 1:30).

"I will remove the iniquity of that land in one day." Has that happened in our day? No, it certainly has not happened yet. But it will happen in the future. When the Lord Jesus Christ comes, He will remove the iniquity of Israel in one day.

> In that day, saith the Lord of hosts, shall ye call every man his neighbour under the vine and under the fig tree [Zech. 3:10].

"In that day" refers to the Day of the Lord. "Shall ye call every man his neighbour under the vine and under the fig tree" means that they will be dwelling in peace and enjoyment in that day.

CHAPTER 4

THEME: Vision of the lampstand and two olive trees

We have come now to Zechariah's seventh vision. Thinking back over the visions he has had, we can see a story unfolding. He has seen (1) the riders under the myrtle trees, (2) the four horns, (3) the four smiths or carpenters, (4) the man with the measuring line, (5) Joshua and Satan, and then (6) the Branch and the Stone with seven eyes in it. The first four visions symbolize the outward deliverance from the slavery and oppression of Babylon. The visions also look to the end times when Israel again will be scattered throughout the world, as they are today, then returned to their land when the Lord Jesus brings them back.

The fifth and sixth visions symbolized inner salvation. The high priest Joshua, clothed in dirty garments which God replaced with clean garments, tells the story of a people brought back to the land for a purpose, but they can't be used in their sin. They will have to be cleansed; but they cannot cleanse themselves, and their religion won't do it. The cleansing has to come from someone outside themselves. "Come now, and let us reason together, saith the LORD: though your sins be as scarlet, they shall be as white as snow; though they be red like crimson, they shall be as wool" (Isa. 1:18). God Himself provides the redemption ". . . with the precious blood of Christ, as of a lamb without blemish and without spot" (1 Pet. 1:19). The cleansing is actually salvation—"Not by works of righteousness which we have done, but according to his mercy he saved us, by the washing of regeneration, and renewing of the Holy Ghost" (Titus 3:5).

Now that Joshua, the high priest, is cleansed, you may think that he is ready for service. No, he is not quite ready. We come now to the vision of the golden lampstand, which is going to show us *how* Joshua is to fulfill the office of high priest.

VISION OF THE LAMPSTAND
AND TWO OLIVE TREES

And the angel that talked with me came again, and waked me, as a man that is wakened out of his sleep [Zech. 4:1].

Let me call your attention again to the fact that Zechariah was awake when he received these visions. At this point he already has had six tremendous visions. He was working the swing shift and the night shift and it was time to have a little rest. So after he had been given the sixth vision, he dozed off. Now the angel has to wake him up because he is not to be given this vision in a dream; he will *see* every bit of it.

And said unto me, What seest thou? And I said, I have looked, and behold a candlestick all of gold, with a bowl upon the top of it, and his seven lamps thereon, and seven pipes to the seven lamps, which are upon the top thereof [Zech. 4:2].

The word *candlestick* in the Authorized Version is properly translated "lampstand" because this is the seven-branched lampstand which stood in the Holy Place of the tabernacle and later in the temple, and in our day it is one of the symbols of the nation Israel. There are other symbols of this nation which are used in Scripture, such as the burning bush, the vine, and the olive tree, but here it is the menorah, the lampstand.

In the tabernacle, and later in the temple, the seven-branched lampstand was the most beautiful of the pieces of furniture. It was handwrought of solid gold. Bezaleel, the skilled artisan, was the one who fashioned it originally. There were three branches going out on each side of the main stem, and on top of each were bowls beautifully made like open almond flowers in which the lamps were placed. The high priest had charge of the lampstand. He would light the lamps and keep them filled with oil. Also it was his business to trim the wicks and to see that they burned continually. In the Book of Revelation we have a picture of the Lord Jesus Christ, our Great High Priest, walking in the middle of the lampstands which represented the seven churches in Asia Minor. He warned them that if they didn't repent of their sins He would remove their lampstands. And He did just that. In modern Turkey today not one of those churches is in existence. They all lie in ruins. Christ removed their lampstands. And in our own land our Great High Priest has closed the door of many a church which was not giving out the Word of God. Our Lord has a snuffer, and He just snuffs them out.

And here in Zechariah's vision the picture is of the nation Israel, represented by the menorah, which will in the future become a witness for God in the world.

"With a bowl upon the top of it." This is something new which is added that you don't find in the instructions given to Moses for fashioning the original lampstand. Here there is a "bowl" which acts as a reservoir or oil tank over the seven lamps so that the oil flows by gravity into the lamps from the elevated bowl. The oil is the all–important factor in the vision.

The lampstand speaks of Christ; the lamps with the oil in them speak of the Holy Spirit. We have no better picture of the Holy Spirit than the oil of the lampstand. Hengstenberg is correct in saying that "oil is one of the most clearly defined symbols in the Bible," and the symbolism is that of the Holy Spirit. While the oil represents the Holy Spirit, the light which is given out represents Christ because He is the Light of the World. The lampstand probably presents the most complete picture of Christ that the symbolism of the tabernacle gives to us. The measurement of the lampstand was not given because it is impossible to measure deity. It was fashioned in a very wonderful way with open almond blossoms at the top into which the little lamps were placed after they had been filled with oil and their wicks trimmed.

When the Lord Jesus was preparing to leave this earth, He told His disciples that He would send the Holy Spirit, adding, "Howbeit when he, the Spirit of truth, is come, he will guide you into all truth: for he shall not speak of himself; but whatsoever he shall hear, that shall he speak. . . . He shall glorify me: for he shall receive of mine, and shall shew it unto you" (John 16:13-14). With that in mind, look at the lampstand. The lampstand supported the lamps with the light shining from them, and the light, in turn, revealed the beauty and glory of the lampstand. In just such a way, the Holy Spirit does not speak of Himself, but He reveals the glories and the beauties of the Lord Jesus Christ.

> **And two olive trees by it, one upon the right side of the bowl, and the other upon the left side thereof [Zech. 4:3].**

The two olive trees were identified in Zechariah's day. Zerubbabel, who was the king in the line of David, is one of the olive trees. The other olive tree was Joshua, the high priest. They would be the two instruments God would use to bring light back into the nation Israel and to make them a light to the world.

The olive oil, as I have already indicated (the word in the Hebrew is beautiful: *golden oil*), represents the Holy Spirit. This prophecy is also destined for a future day, the Great Tribulation period. This is clearly identified for us in the Book of Revelation: "And I will give power unto my two witnesses, and they shall prophesy a thousand two hundred and threescore days, clothed in sackcloth. These are the two olive trees, and the two candlesticks [lampstands] standing before the God of the earth" (Rev. 11:3-4). Out yonder in the Great Tribulation period there will be no witness on the earth because the Antichrist, with the power of Satan (since God withdraws His hand for that brief moment), will have stopped the mouth of every witness on the topside of the earth—with the exception of two. God says that always in the mouth of two witnesses a thing is established. Also God says He will never leave Himself without a witness. During that period there will be these two men who will witness for Him. Who they are is speculation. I think Elijah may be one of them, but whether the other is Enoch, whether he is Moses, whether he is John the Baptist, or somebody else, I do not know. But their identity is not the important thing. God will have two witnesses, and they will speak in the power of the Holy Spirit in that day. They will be God's witnesses. That is His promise for the future just as He used Zerubbabel and Joshua in Zechariah's day.

Let me say again that the visions of Zechariah are like stepping-stones which tell out a story. They reveal a very beautiful and complete picture when we put them together. God gave these to the returned remnant for their encouragement. The children of Israel had been in Babylonian captivity and now had returned to the land of Israel. God had made it clear to them that all of this had happened according to His plan and purpose. Now back in the land, they had to be cleansed from their sins and brought into a right relationship with God so that they could render an effective testimony for Him.

Although these visions of Zechariah had a local fulfillment for the past, they also looked forward to the future. The *complete* fulfillment will be during the millennial period when God will return the Jewish people to the land of Israel. And God will cleanse them in that future day. In chapter 13 of Zechariah we will find that a foundation will be opened for the cleansing of David's offspring and for the inhabitants of Jerusalem. After they have been cleansed, they will become a light to the world—which was God's original intention for them. In Deuteronomy 32:8 we read this remarkable verse: "When the Most High divided to the nations their inheritance, when he separated the sons of Adam, he set the bounds of the people according to the number of the children of Israel." Why did He arrange the nations according to the number of the children of Israel? The reason is that God intended them to be His witnesses.

The land of Israel is a very sensitive piece of real estate. God has chosen it and made it that way. He chose it because it was the very center of the three major continents: Africa, Asia, and Europe. It is right on the crossroads of those three continents. There is no place on earth that is more sensitive or that has caused more international problems than that little spot. I think that God intended that it should be that way. And there will be trouble until Israel becomes the center for the proclamation of the Word of God. In Ezekiel 5:5 we read these words: "Thus saith the Lord God; This is Jerusalem: I have set it in the midst of the nations and countries that are round about her." Why? So she could be a witness. And in that future day they will be a witness in every corner and crevice of this world.

It is interesting that the popular symbol of Israel today is the menorah. When I have visited in Israel, the fig tree, the vine, and the olive tree symbols have not been in evidence, but I have seen the menorah in many places. I was there during their twenty-fifth anniversary, and I saw the menorah symbol everywhere. Someday the people of Israel will be the witness which God intended them to be.

Israel has failed in the past, but the church is failing in the present. Although Christ has commanded us to go into all the world with the gospel, there are many places in the world that have no witness at all. I am delighted to be penetrating some of those unreached places by means of radio. A letter came to me from South America telling of a young man who had come to know Christ through listening to the Bible teaching by radio, and he immediately became the preacher to his village. Why? Because there wasn't any preacher there, and he was the only witness in the town. He became a flaming evangel, a light for the Lord in that place.

In that future day the Jewish people will be witnesses in every corner of the world, and the Word of God shall go out from Jerusalem. "And it shall come to pass in the last days, that the mountain of the Lord's house shall be established in the top of the mountains, and shall be exalted above the hills; and all nations shall flow unto it. And many people shall go and say, Come ye, and let us go up to the mountain of the Lord, to the house of the God of Jacob; and he will teach us of his ways, and we will walk in his paths: for out of Zion shall go forth the law, and the word of the Lord from Jerusalem" (Isa. 2:2–3).

> **So I answered and spake to the angel that talked with me, saying, What are these, my lord? [Zech. 4:4].**

This young man Zechariah has no inhibitions, so he says, "I see these things, but what is the meaning of them?"

> Then the angel that talked with me answered and said
> unto me, Knowest thou not what these be? And I said,
> No, my lord [Zech. 4:5].

The answer of the angel implies that Zechariah should know what it means. In effect he is saying, "You ought to be able to understand it. You are looking at the golden lampstand, and you ought to know the meaning of that." Well, Zechariah didn't. He said, "No, my lord, I don't understand it at all."

> Then he answered and spake unto me, saying, This is
> the word of the LORD unto Zerubbabel, saying, Not by
> might, nor by power, but by my spirit, saith the LORD of
> hosts [Zech. 4:6].

Notice that this is God's message to Zerubbabel. Now who is Zerubbabel? He is serving as the civil head of Jerusalem (while Joshua is serving as the religious head). He was the head of the tribe of Judah at the time of their return to Jerusalem after the seventy-year Babylonian captivity. He is the one who led the first group of his people back to their homeland, as described in the Book of Ezra. Zerubbabel's great work was that of rebuilding the temple, but the work was dogged by danger from the outside and discouragement from within. God is giving this vision to strengthen the faith of Zerubbabel. It has real meaning for him, and also it contains a great principle for you and me.

Here is the message: "Not by might, nor by power, but by my spirit, saith the LORD of hosts." The words *might* and *power* are quite interesting. *Might* is a general word for human resources such as physical strength, human ability or efficiency, or wealth. *Power* also denotes mere human strength—physical, material, and mental strength. Therefore, let me give you my translation of this verse: "It is not by brawn nor by brains, but by my spirit, saith the LORD of hosts." You can see that this would be a great encouragement to Zerubbabel, the civil ruler. He and Joshua, the religious ruler, were represented by the two olive trees who were supplying oil to the lampstand. The message is simply this: It will not be by your cleverness, you ability, or your physical strength that the temple will be rebuilt, but by the spirit of God.

My friend, if the spirit of God is not in our enterprises today, they will come to naught because God is not carrying on His work by our brain or brawn. We speak of clever preachers who deliver very well-composed sermons and all of that, but God's work is not carried on that way. Sometimes a clever preacher is a dangerous man. The fellow who is sharp mentally may be sharp in the wrong direction and cause a great deal of difficulty among God's people. I have had to stand on the sidelines and see a great deal of religious racketeering going on when I couldn't lift my voice against it without being misunderstood. It is quite evident that some clever fellows were good backslappers, good public relations men, good administrators, had nice personalities and a great deal of charisma, and they made an appeal. But God does not carry on His work by the human instrument. It is "not by might nor by power"; it is not by brain nor by brawn, but it is "by my spirit, saith the LORD."

Let me be personal and very frank. Anything that Vernon McGee does in the flesh, that is by his own effort, God hates. He can't use it. It will come to nothing because it is nothing in the world but Vernon McGee building a haystack which ultimately is going to be consumed by fire. God wants to do His work through us, be the power of the Holy Spirit. This is important for us to see.

Now looking into the future, this will be especially true during the Millennium. Again, it will not be by brain or by brawn, "but by my spirit, saith the LORD." David Baron has put it like this: "It is in His light, and by means of the golden oil of His Spirit, which shall then be shed upon them abundantly, that Israel's candlestick shall yet shine with a sevenfold brilliancy for the illumination of all the nations of the earth." That, my friend, is a great statement.

Back in the days of Zechariah there was a remnant that needed this encouragement because they were overwhelmed by opposition, and they were beset by doubts and by fears. So the vision was given—it is the Word of the Lord unto Zerubbabel—to encourage them.

Who art thou, O great mountain? before Zerubbabel thou shalt become a plain: and he shall bring forth the

> headstone thereof with shoutings, crying, Grace, grace
> unto it [Zech. 4:7].

"Who art thou, O great mountain?" The mountain represents opposition. This vision encourages them to believe that Zerubbabel will be able to remove the mountain of opposition. The Lord Jesus used "mountain" in that sense. The Lord Jesus said to His disciples, ". . . If ye have faith as a grain of mustard seed, ye shall say unto this mountain, Remove hence to yonder place; and it shall remove; and nothing shall be impossible unto you" (Matt. 17:20). I don't think our Lord was speaking of removing physical mountains—we don't know of any physical mountains being moved in that day—but the faith that removes mountains is the faith that removes obstacles and opposition to the work of God. And that is the picture this vision gives. God's temple will be rebuilt regardless of the seeming impossibilities.

"And he shall bring forth the headstone thereof with shoutings, crying, Grace, grace unto it." The headstone is the finishing or gable stone which marks the completion of a building. He is saying that the temple will be completed with the shoutings and cheers of the people. What an encouragement this was to the disheartened remnant!

> Moreover the word of the LORD came unto me, saying,
>
> The hands of Zerubbabel have laid the foundation of this house; his hands shall also finish it; and thou shalt know that the LORD of hosts hath sent me unto you [Zech. 4:8–9].

This is God's promise that the work won't drag on and finally be completed by someone else, but that Zerubbabel himself is going to finish it. It reminds me of the promise in the New Testament: "Being confident of this very thing, that he which hath begun a good work in you will perform it until the day of Jesus Christ" (Phil. 1:6). God is saying to Zerubbabel, "You have laid the foundation, and I was with you. Well, you are going to put the roof on it, too, and I will be with you."

> For who hath despised the day of small things? for they
> shall rejoice, and shall see the plummet in the hand of
> Zerubbabel with those seven; they are the eyes of the
> LORD, which run to and fro through the whole earth
> [Zech. 4:10].

"For who hath despised the day of small things?" I can tell you who
has—*we* despise the day of small things. We Americans are impressed
with the big and brassy. We like our Christian work to be a success
story. And we measure success by the size of the building and the
crowds that come to it. Well, I am becoming more and more convinced that the Lord is working in quiet ways and in quiet places today. I am talking to myself when I say that we should quit despising
small things.

"For they shall rejoice, and shall see the plummet in the hand of
Zerubbabel with those seven." The "plummet" or "plumb" is a weight
on the end of a string, and it is used to determine if a building is
vertical to the earth. I wish I had thought of using a plummet when I
put up a little shed on my place—because it isn't quite straight.

"They are the eyes of the LORD, which run to and fro through the
whole earth" indicates that God knows what is going on, and He is
still overruling.

> Then answered I, and said unto him, What are these
> two olive trees upon the right side of the candlestick and
> upon the left side thereof?
>
> And I answered again, and said unto him, What be
> these two olive branches which through the two golden
> pipes empty the golden oil out of themselves?
>
> And he answered me and said, knowest thou not what
> these be? And I said, No, my lord [Zech. 4:11–13].

Zechariah is asking again for an explanation. And the angel's answer,
"Knowest thou not what these be?" implies that he *ought* to know. But
he doesn't know.

**Then said he, These are the two anointed ones, that
stand by the Lord of the whole earth [Zech. 4:14].**

These are the two Spirit-filled men, Zerubbabel, the civil ruler, and
Joshua, the religious ruler. We have already seen that Joshua, representing the nation, has been cleansed and now stands in clean garments. When the remnant of Israel confessed their sin and accepted
God's redemption, they were cleansed and now stand in the righteousness of Christ. Therefore, they can be Spirit-filled and can be
used of God.

This has a message for you and for me. God wants to fill us with
the Holy Spirit. But there are certain conditions to be met. Two of
them are negative: (1) ". . . grieve not the holy Spirit of God, whereby
ye are sealed unto the day of redemption" (Eph. 4:30). We cannot be
filled with the Spirit if there is sin in our lives—we have to be *clean* in
God's sight. (2) "Quench not the Spirit" (1 Thess. 5:19). Quenching
the Spirit is being out of the will of God. And when we are out of the
will of God, God cannot use us. If God wants you in Africa and you
are still in your homeland, I don't think God is going to use you here.
But, my friend, if you are in Africa and God wants you to be in your
own country, He won't use you there either. The third condition to be
met for the filling of the Spirit is positive: (3) ". . . Walk in the
Spirit . . ." (Gal. 5:16). Walking in the Spirit is a very practical sort of
thing. It is to walk by means of the Spirit, to rest on Him, depending
upon Him to do what we cannot do ourselves.

The vision of the lampstand was an encouragement to the remnant
in Zechariah's day; it has an application to our day; and it looks forward to the day when God will pour out His Spirit without measure. I
see very little of a genuine pouring out of His Spirit in our contemporary society, but during the Millennium He is going to pour out His
Spirit upon *all* flesh. That day is yet future, my friend.

CHAPTER 5

THEME: *Vision of the flying roll; vision of a woman in an ephah*

We come now to the two visions which are the most highly symbolic and unusual of this series of visions. The first, the flying roll or scroll, marks a sharp division in the meaning of the visions which Zechariah received. In the first two chapters God makes it clear that He intends to put down all the enemies of Israel and that the nation will become the nation of priests which was God's original intention. God told them that this was His desire for them when He brought them out of Egyptian bondage, but, because of their sin, only one tribe—the tribe of Levi—was chosen for the priesthood. Then in the vision of Joshua and Satan we learned that the nation first had to be cleansed. Then the vision of the branch and the stone with seven eyes looked forward to the Kingdom Age when God, having cleansed them, would use them, and they would become a light to the world, symbolized by the lampstand being fed oil from the olive trees. The oil, representing the Holy Spirit, signified that they would witness in the power of the Holy Spirit.

That is all well and good, but it does raise a question. Does it mean that every member of this nation, every Israelite, will be chosen—even those who live in continual rebellion and sin? In the visions before us, we will see that the judgment of God will come upon those who do *not* become obedient unto Him. He will ferret out those who are rebellious, and He will judge them.

By the same token, God will do this in the whole world. Although these visions have in mind the local nation, they also have a world view. There is here a global gospel that looks forward to the establishment of God's Kingdom here upon the earth. This makes very clear the thing that God said regarding Israel: ". . . For they are not all Israel, which are of Israel" (Rom. 9:6). It is the national unity, the corporate body—not every member—that will be accepted. Each individual will have to be obedient to God, come God's way for cleansing, as we have seen, and will have to receive the Messiah.

What is said of the nation Israel is also true of the church. Not every church member is a genuine Christian—that is, a member of the body of believers which is called the church. There will come a day when there will be a separation of believers and unbelievers. The great division of the church will be at the Rapture, and the division for Israel and for all the nations on the earth will be at the second coming of Christ when He gathers His elect into His Kingdom. Then there will be a judgment, and Satan will be bound for one thousand years. All of this is in the picture that is given to us here. You can see that this was for the encouragement of the godly remnant of Israel in Zechariah's day as well as for us today.

VISION OF THE FLYING ROLL

Then I turned, and lifted up mine eyes, and looked, and behold a flying roll [Zech. 5:1].

The first thing that we should establish is that this flying roll is a scroll which represents the Word of God. We get this explanation from the prophet Ezekiel. "And when I looked, behold, an hand was sent unto me; and, lo, a roll of a book was therein; and he spread it before me; and it was written within and without: and there was written therein lamentations, and mourning, and woe. Moreover he said unto me, Son of man, eat that thou findest; eat this roll, and go speak unto the house of Israel. So I opened my mouth, and he caused me to eat that roll. And he said unto me, Son of man, cause thy belly to eat, and fill thy bowels with this roll that I give thee. Then did I eat it; and it was in my mouth as honey for sweetness. And he said unto me, Son of man, go, get thee unto the house of Israel, and speak with my words unto them" (Ezek. 2:9—3:4). Ezekiel was to digest the Word of God and then he was to give it out to the people. This is a tremendous picture for us who are preachers. We ought to digest the Word of God. It might be bitter in our tummies, but in our mouths it should be as sweet as honey—that is, something that we delight in giving out.

I should add that there is a great difference of opinion and many interpretations regarding the meaning of the flying scroll. But the solid interpretation which has come down through the centuries is that the scroll represents the Word of God in general and the Ten Commandments in particular.

> **And he said unto me, What seest thou? And I answered,
> I see a flying roll; the length thereof is twenty cubits,
> and the breadth thereof ten cubits [Zech. 5:2].**

The size of the scroll was twenty cubits by ten cubits—that's a very large scroll. The scrolls in the days of Zechariah were made of papyrus or animal skins with a roller at each end so that the ones reading could roll it off one roller and onto the other roller as they read it. Instead of turning pages as we do when we read a book, they would unroll more of the scroll as they read along. But the scroll of Zechariah's vision was 20x10 cubits (a cubit was the measurement from the end of the middle finger to the elbow and would vary depending upon the size of the individual but was about eighteen inches), which would make the scroll about 15x30 feet, much larger than a bed sheet, even a king-sized sheet. The only way it could be seen would be spread out, and he sees it as a great *flying* scroll, that is, traveling rapidly over the whole land. I imagine that it was completely unrolled as it moved over the earth.

The size of the scroll is probably significant as it is the same size as the Holy Place of the tabernacle and of the Porch of Solomon in the temple. "And the porch before the temple of the house, twenty cubits was the length thereof, according to the breadth of the house; and ten cubits was the breadth thereof before the house" (1 Kings 6:3). That was the place where the priest could come and worship according to the Law. No one could ever go inside the veil unless the blood was put in there. That was done by the high priest only once a year when he went in as a representative of the whole nation. When the high priest went in there, he stood on redeemed ground, having been redeemed by the blood.

You and I today stand on redeemed ground. We have not been redeemed by gold and silver or by any precious stones or precious jewels, but by the precious blood of Christ. You and I are not standing on a flying carpet. We do not rest on a missile sent from heaven. We have been delivered from the penalty and the power of sin. "And as Moses lifted up the serpent in the wilderness, even so must the Son of man be lifted up: that whosoever believeth in him should not perish, but have eternal life" (John 3:14–15).

> **Then said he unto me, This is the curse that goeth forth over the face of the whole earth: for every one that stealeth shall be cut off as on this side according to it; and every one that sweareth shall be cut off as on that side according to it [Zech. 5:3].**

Apparently the Ten Commandments were written on the scroll, and the Ten Commandments were divided into two parts. The first four commandments deal with man's relationship to God, and the last six commandments deal with man's relationship to man. Therefore, the commandment regarding stealing cited here, "for every one that stealeth shall be cut off as on this side according to it," probably represents the section which deals with man's relationship to man. This is clearly identified in Psalm 50: "When thou sawest a thief, then thou consentedst with him [Thou shalt not steal], and hast been partaker with adulterers [Thou shalt not commit adultery]. Thou givest thy mouth to evil, and thy tongue frameth deceit. Thou sittest and speakest against thy brother; thou slanderest thine own mother's son [Thou shalt not bear false witness against thy neighbour]. These things hast thou done, and I kept silence; thou thoughtest that I was altogether such as one as thyself: but I will reprove thee, and set them in order before thine eyes" (Ps. 50:18–21). Now, because men in that day were able to break the Ten Commandments without suffering God's punishment, they came to the conclusion that He was just like they were and would not do anything about their transgressions. But God says that He is going to do something about them.

The Mosaic Law was given to the nation of Israel, and it was to be the *Law* of that nation, and they were to obey the Law. Well, they disobeyed it, of course, and so God put them out of their land. And in their dispersion among the nations, they scattered the Mosaic Law. The mark of civilization has been the commandments of God which relate especially to man's relationship with man.

I want you to notice here the great principle which is put down concerning the Law and especially the Ten Commandments. The Ten Commandments were given to the nation Israel as they stood in the crossroads of the world, and they took them with them wherever they went. They had a tremendous influence upon Egypt as they became a nation down there. When they went into Assyrian and Babylonian captivity, they had a great influence upon those first great empires. They had an influence upon the Graeco-Macedonian Empire and the Roman Empire.

The Ten Commandments produced a civilization. You can say what you please, but the great civilizations of this world have had these laws as a basis: Thou shalt not kill. Thou shalt not steal. Thou shalt not bear false witness. Thou shalt not commit adultery. These have been basic to a nation, building the homes, building a way of life, and establishing a civilization. As long as our nation had them as bedrock, we were blessed of God, and our problems were few compared to what they are today. But our contemporary world society has abandoned them, and we have come to the same place to which the nation Israel had come. God has given Israel as an example. God is saying, "Although I have chosen Israel as a nation, I will judge every individual that breaks My Commandments." And so this flying scroll represents for the whole earth the basis upon which God deals with nations. The interesting thing is that it is very difficult to find anything wrong with the Law.

Now God goes ahead and says this—

> I will bring it forth, saith the LORD of hosts, and it shall enter into the house of the thief, and into the house of him that sweareth falsely by my name: and it shall remain in the midst of his house, and shall consume it with the timber thereof and the stones thereof [Zech. 5:4].

"It shall enter into the house of the thief"—that represents the commandments which have to do with man's relationship to man.

"And into the house of him that sweareth falsely by my name" refers to the first section of the Ten Commandments. Even by the name of God a man would perjure himself!

The Ten Commandments were never given to the Christian as a way of life. We as believers have been called to a much higher plane, and we attain that plane by grace. Actually, man cannot even attain the plane of the Mosaic Law unaided. God gave them the Law, but He gave them no aid to go with it. That is, He did not give them the filling of the Spirit; the Holy Spirit did not indwell the Old Testament saints. Therefore man in his own strength and ability could never measure up to the Ten Commandments. You and I live in the dispensation of grace, and God has given to us the Holy Spirit whereby we can produce the fruit of the Spirit in our lives (love, joy, peace, longsuffering, etc.), which were never in the Mosaic Law.

VISION OF A WOMAN IN AN EPHAH

Suppose I told you that last night a missile from outer space landed in my backyard and two little men in green came out of it and talked with me. Would you believe it? Well, if you won't, I won't tell you such a thing. But there are intelligent people today (as well as others) who actually believe in flying saucers. Some have even testified to having seen them. They have even said they saw little people inside. I understand the U.S. Navy has been giving this serious investigation over the years. We hear from two groups. One believes sincerely and vociferously that there are flying saucers. The other group doubts it and denies it equally vociferously.

While I was a pastor in downtown Los Angeles, I had an invitation to go out to Apple Valley to a large rock that is out in that desert area, which was declared to be the landing field where the missiles from outer space came in. I was told they would give me a ride in one of the flying saucers. I didn't go out there for two reasons. One was that I wasn't sure there were flying saucers out there—I'm very much of a skeptic. The other reason was that I was afraid if I did go out there and they put me in one of them, they would take me off and not bring me back—no one assured me of a round-trip ticket. So I didn't go out there. I voiced my skepticism and cynicism about the whole business, but there were some who sincerely believed that missiles from outer space were landing and taking off out in that area. I have driven by that location many times since then, and I don't know why, but I always pick up speed going by that big rock!

Zechariah didn't believe in flying saucers either, but he saw two flying objects in his visions. He saw some strange missiles from outer space. Remember that I said at the beginning that the Book of Zechariah is one of the apocalyptic books of the Bible. It is ethereal, seraphic, spiritual, and highly symbolic. In other words, what he writes is out of this world. We need to avoid fanaticism on one hand and materialism on the other hand.

We're at the launching pad, and we are ready to see another vision. Actually, we are going to see the first astronaut. Believe it or not, we will learn that it is a woman who is in one of those capsules. It is called an ephah or a bushel basket.

> **Then the angel that walked with me went forth, and said unto me, Lift up now thine eyes, and see what is this that goeth forth [Zech. 5:5].**

Again he has his eyes wide open—this is no dream. And the interpreting angel says, "Look up, please."

> **And I said, What is it? And he said, This is an ephah that goeth forth. He said moreover, This is their resemblance through all the earth [Zech. 5:6].**

"And I said, What is it?" After all, this is the first astronaut Zechariah had ever seen, and he didn't know what it was. Possibly you can remember the great thrill it was when you heard about Alan Shepard making his trip in space. He didn't get very far, but he was the first American in space. Well, here is a woman in space, and Zechariah wants an explanation.

"This is an ephah that goeth forth." An ephah is a dry measure equal to a little more than a bushel. It was used to measure such commodities as flour and barley; therefore, this symbolized trade or commerce.

> **And, behold, there was lifted up a talent of lead: and this is a woman that sitteth in the midst of the ephah [Zech. 5:7].**

What we have in this vision is a continuation of judgment upon the sin and iniquity of Israel. It looks forward to the Millennium where sin and iniquity will be removed from the land. Also, it looks forward to the judgment of Babylon, which will precede the Millennium. We need to compare it with Revelation 18 where we see the judgment of commercial Babylon. (Revelation 17 pictures the judgment of religious Babylon.) God will judge this matter of covetousness. His command is, "Thou shalt not covet." And God will judge the love of money and the greed that are connected with commercialism. The "talent" was the largest measure of weight, and it was made of lead, the most common heavy metal which was employed in all commercial transactions for weighing out money.

We find that one of the great sins of the Israelites when they returned from Babylon was an insatiable love for money and desire for material things. You may recall that Nehemiah had to deal with them on this issue because they were lending to their brothers at high rates of interest (usury). They had been forbidden by the Mosaic Law to do this, and Nehemiah really straightened them out. The last book of the Old Testament, Malachi, pictures life in the land after the temple had been built. Malachi asks the question, "Will a man rob God? . . ." (Mal. 3:8). Believe me, God answered that question. He said that the whole nation had robbed Him. You see, they were guilty of covetousness; they were bent on accumulating riches for themselves, and they were willing to rob God and hurt their brother in order to do it. That is what they were doing in Zechariah's day, and God is revealing to him that He intends to remove that spirit of covetousness from the land.

"This is a woman that sitteth in the midst of the ephah." Anytime in the Scriptures that we see a woman out of place, there is an evil connotation. For example, the woman in the parable the Lord Jesus gave (see Matt. 13:33) who put leaven in flour. That leaven represents evil, and the leaven of evil is a principle all the way through the Word of God. And when Scripture pictures a woman in religion, such as the church at Thyatira which had ". . . that woman Jezebel, which calleth herself a prophetess . . ." (Rev. 2:20), and the "great whore" of Revelation 17, she represents evil. In Zechariah's vision, the woman represents the nation of Israel that had gone into commercialism. God wants to bless them, but their awful sin of covetousness must be dealt with first.

> And he said, This is wickedness. And he cast it into the midst of the ephah; and he cast the weight of lead upon the mouth thereof [Zech. 5:8].

Let me give you Merrill Unger's translation and amplification of this verse (pp. 96–97):

> Having announced concerning the woman, This is wickedness, thereupon he [the interpreting angel] cast her [the woman] into the middle of the ephah and cast the lead stone [weight] upon its mouth [opening]. . . . She has been all along sitting or dwelling in the ephah, contentedly, but now that the time has come for commercial Babylon to be removed, to be destroyed, the woman tries to escape from it because she does not want to be removed with it, and so share its inevitable fate. Therefore, she tries to escape.

> Then lifted I up mine eyes, and looked, and, behold, there came out two women, and the wind was in their wings; for they had wings like the wings of a stork: and they lifted up the ephah between the earth and the heaven [Zech. 5:9].

Some time ago a movie was produced called "The Flying Nun"; so I call these two women the two flying nuns. But what do they represent? Well, we may be sure that they represent agents of evil because they are associated with and protective of the woman in the ephah—and the angel had said of her, "This is wickedness."

"They had wings like the wings of a stork"—that is, powerful wings. In Scripture the stork is not a picture of an angel. It is a dirty bird, an unclean bird.

> **Then said I to the angel that talked with me, Whither do these bear the ephah?**
>
> **And he said unto me, To build it an house in the land of Shinar: and it shall be established, and set there upon her own base [Zech. 5:10–11].**

God is moving this matter of godless and heartless commercialism out of the land of Palestine.

Now I want you to see something here. The children of Israel were originally a pastoral and agricultural people, and most of the Mosaic Law has to do with that type of life-style. It gives instructions regarding the land itself, the vineyards, the grain, the livestock, and all that sort of thing. And in our day, the Jews who have returned to Palestine have returned, in a large measure, to the soil. However, when they are out of that land, they get into other businesses. I have never heard of a Jewish farmer in America, have you?

When they were in Babylonian captivity, they learned commercialism, and they learned it from the Gentiles. They became good businessmen, and they acquired an insatiable love for riches which they saw among the Gentiles in Babylon.

Let me refer you again to the Book of Revelation where, in chapter 18, we find that God is going to judge commercial Babylon at the setting up of His Kingdom; in fact, He is going to get rid of it.

My friend, the Bible is a rather revolutionary book, which may be one reason why some people don't like it. It is said that John Calvin got capitalism from the Bible; and I think that he did. But I want to remind you that there is a great deal more in the Bible on the side of the poor people than on the side of the rich. In the Epistle of James, we find this harsh condemnation: "Go to now, ye rich men, weep and howl for your miseries that shall come upon you. Your riches are corrupted, and your garments are motheaten. Your gold and silver is cankered; and the rust of them shall be a witness against you, and shall eat your flesh as it were fire. Ye have heaped treasure together for the last days" (James 5:1–3). He speaks out against the gathering of money just for the sake of gathering it. Then he goes on, "Behold, the hire of the labourers who have reaped down your fields, which is of you kept back by fraud, crieth: and the cries of them which have reaped are entered into the ears of the Lord of sabaoth" (James 5:4).

I wonder what God has to say to some of these great corporations and the great labor unions of our contemporary society. That sort of thing is not going into the Kingdom of God upon this earth. God is going to judge it and get rid of it. If there ever was a revolutionary book, it is this Book, the Word of God. It is too hot for a lot of folk to handle!

Now notice that Zechariah asks the interpreting angel, "Whither do these bear the ephah?" And the angel answered, "To build it an house in the land of Shinar." Where is Shinar? It is the land of Babylon. God will return this evil system to the place it came from, and its final destruction was seen by the apostle John: "And after these things I saw another angel come down from heaven, having great power; and the earth was lightened with his glory. And he cried mightily with a strong voice, saying, Babylon the great is fallen, is fallen, and is become the habitation of devils, and the hold of every foul spirit, and a cage of every unclean and hateful bird. For all nations have drunk of the wine of the wrath of her fornication, and the kings of the earth have committed fornication with her, and the merchants of the earth are waxed rich through the abundance of her delicasies. And I heard another voice from heaven, saying, Come out of her, my people, that ye be not partakers of her sins, and that ye receive not of her plagues. For her sins have reached unto heaven, and God hath remembered her iniquities" (Rev. 18:1–5).

My friend, in our contemporary civilization, is God in big business? Is God in the stock market? Is God in the labor unions? Is God in the entertainment business? Anyone with any intelligence recognizes that God is left out of all of them. And God intends to remove them from the earth someday. "And a mighty angel took up a stone like a great millstone, and cast it into the sea, saying, Thus with violence shall that great city Babylon be thrown down, and shall be found no more at all. And the voice of harpers, and musicians, and of pipers, and trumpeters, shall be heard no more at all in thee; and no craftsman, of whatsoever craft he be, shall be found any more in thee; and the sound of a millstone shall be heard no more at all in thee; and the light of a candle shall shine no more at all in thee; and the voice of the bridegroom and of the bride shall be heard no more at all in thee: for thy merchants were the great men of the earth; for by thy sorceries were all nations deceived. And in her was found the blood of prophets, and of saints, and of all that were slain upon the earth" (Rev. 18:21–24, italics mine).

When this evil system is removed, Palestine will become truly the holy land; and when wickedness is destroyed from the whole earth, the Kingdom of God will come to the earth. What a glorious prospect this is as you and I live in this present evil age!

CHAPTER 6

THEME: Vision of the four chariots; the symbolic crowning of Joshua

We come now to the final vision of the ten which were given to Zechariah in one night. To get them before us as a background, let me enumerate them again: (1) The riders under the myrtle trees; (2) the four horns; (3) the four smiths; (4) the man with the measuring line; (5) Joshua and Satan; (6) the Branch and the Stone with seven eyes; (7) the lampstand and the two olive trees; (8) the flying scroll; and (9) the woman in the ephah; and now the tenth, the four chariots. Let me say again that some expositors find only eight visions in this series, but I believe that it is highly consistent to see the visions as ten.

VISION OF THE FOUR CHARIOTS

> And I turned, and lifted up mine eyes, and looked, and, behold, there came four chariots out from between two mountains; and the mountains were mountains of brass [Zech. 6:1].

"I . . . lifted up mine eyes, and looked" indicates again that his eyes were wide open; he saw these things—this was not a dream.

"Two mountains; and the mountains were mountains of brass." The majority of the outstanding commentators agree that these two mountains are Mount Zion and the Mount of Olives, which would locate these four chariots down in the Kidron Valley.

"There came four chariots"—we assume that horses were hitched to the chariots and there were charioteers or drivers for each of them. As we read on, we will find that this is true. These chariots could be interpreted as representing the four great world empires that Daniel saw in his vision. All of them were gentile empires, and all of them have been judged of God. That part of Daniel's vision has been literally fulfilled. These four chariots could represent that very easily.

However, I am inclined to identify these four chariots with the vision which John saw in the Apocalypse, speaking of that which is yet future. In fact, Revelation 6 opens with John's vision of the Great Tribulation period by presenting to us four horsemen, and there is a striking correspondence between them and Zechariah's vision of the four chariots. We have seen in chapter 5 the visions of judgment primarily with reference to the people of Israel, but here in chapter 6 God's judgment is upon the gentile nations which have oppressed God's people. It reveals not only a past judgment but a future judgment which is to come during the Great Tribulation period.

"And the mountains were mountains of brass." These mountains were of brass, or literally of bronze. Bronze was known in the earth at a very early period. We can go back in history to the Old Stone Age and the New Stone Age, back to the Neolithic and the Paleolithic periods. We find that bronze appears almost at the beginning of civilization.

Symbolically, bronze is used in the Old Testament to represent judgment. It was one of the metals that was used in the tabernacle in the two articles of furniture which were used in the judgment of sin. The brazen altar was made of bronze as was the laver of brass. These both stood in the outer court of the tabernacle, and both had to do with the judgment of the sin of the people.

Since the mountains in this vision are mountains of brass, it would indicate that these mountains speak of judgment. Judgment is going to come forth from God from the Kidron Valley. There are four judgments that go forth, and they are pictured here as four chariots.

> In the first chariot were red horses; and in the second chariot black horses;
>
> And in the third chariot white horses; and in the fourth chariot grisled and bay horses [Zech. 6:2-3].

The colors of these horses are significant. We have the same colors in the four horsemen of the Apocalypse in Revelation 6. I don't think it is accidental that Zechariah had a vision of four chariots and John of four horsemen. They are probably referring to the same events. The red horse in John's vision represents war. The black horse represents famine, and the pale horse is identified as picturing death. All of these picture judgments from almighty God.

Now what does the first horse, the white horse of the Apocalypse, represent? There are white horses here in Zechariah's vision also, which probably symbolize victory. In John's vision, the white horse is immediately followed by the red horse of war. Therefore, I think that the first horseman represents Antichrist and that he will bring a false peace into the world—because after him rides the red horse of war, and war breaks out upon the earth. My friend, I don't think that we have seen an actual *world* war yet; but in the end times the whole earth will be inflamed by war because man is a warlike creature as long as there is sin in his heart. And when that red horseman rides through the earth—I say it reverently—all hell will break loose. It seems to me that no one today is emphasizing how frightful the Great Tribulation is going to be when it breaks upon this earth. Well, it is symbolized by the riding of that red horse of war.

The "grisled and bay horses" of Zechariah's vision are probably more accurately translated as dappled (lit., as if sprinkled with hail) and would correspond to the pale horse of the Apocalypse.

This tenth vision was given to Zechariah for the encouragement of his people, knowing that God would judge the gentile nations as he would judge His own people.

> Then I answered and said unto the angel that talked with me, What are these, my lord?
>
> And the angel answered and said unto me, These are the four spirits of the heavens, which go forth from standing before the Lord of all the earth [Zech. 6:4–5].

"These are the four spirits of the heavens." The "spirits" are obviously angels so that the four chariots are, as David Baron (*The Visions and Prophecies of Zechariah*, p. 175) puts it,

... angelic beings, or heavenly powers—those invisible "messengers" of His "who excel in strength, and who ever stand in His presence, hearkening unto the voice of His word," and then go forth in willing obedience, as swift as the "winds," to carry out His behests (Ps. ciii. 20, 21, civ. 4).

In other words, the angels are in charge of the judgments which will be coming upon the gentile nations, as we see also in the Book of Revelation.

Now we get the interpretation—

> **The black horses which are therein go forth into the north country; and the white go forth after them; and the grisled go forth toward the south country.**
>
> **And the bay went forth, and sought to go that they might walk to and fro through the earth: and he said, Get you hence, walk to and fro through the earth. So they walked to and fro through the earth [Zech. 6:6–7].**

The black and white horses will go forth into the north country. The "grisled" or dappled and "bay" will go forth into the south country.

> **Then cried he upon me, and spake unto me, saying, Behold, these that go toward the north country have quieted my spirit in the north country [Zech. 6:8]**

Notice that none of the horses go to the west—that would put them into the Mediterranean Sea, and none of these are sea horses! Neither do any of the horses go to the east because the great Arabian desert is out there. They go to the north and to the south, which is the way one would go from Israel to any other part of the world. The directions given simply mean that they go out from Israel throughout the whole earth.

It says that the black and the white horses go up into the north country. I personally believe that the judgment of the Great Tribulation period begins with Russia coming down into the land of Israel, so that judgment will first go to the king of the north, to Gog and Magog in the north. Judgment will also go south toward Egypt. However, the riding of the horses is not the main issue here. In the Book of Revelation we are given the series of events in the Great Tribulation period, one event after another, one crisis after another. When the white horse rides forth, he will bring a victory that will set up a false peace upon the earth. The world will think that it is entering the Millennium when actually it will be entering the Great Tribulation period. Immediately after the white horse there will come the red horse of war—war breaks out worldwide—followed by the black horse of famine. Famine generally follows war as do plagues and death, which are symbolized by the fourth, the pale horse. In contrast to this, in the vision of the four chariots which was given to Zechariah, the order is not the important thing. Rather, the emphasis is upon the fact that God intends to judge *all* the nations of the earth, and the four chariots represent those judgments. All of them are to take place during the Tribulation period. This concludes the ten visions given to Zechariah.

THE SYMBOLIC CROWNING OF JOSHUA

Now we come to an event which takes place during the days of Zechariah.

And the word of the LORD came unto me, saying,

Take of them of the captivity, even of Heldai, of Tobijah, and of Jedaiah, which are come from Babylon, and come thou the same day, and go into the house of Josiah the son of Zephaniah [Zech. 6:9–10].

Here we are given the names of three men who came from Babylon. They had not come with either of the two groups of the remnant that returned to the land of Israel, but they came on their own. The name *Heldai* means "robust"; *Tobijah* means "God's goodness"; and *Jedaiah* means "God knows." Linking these names together indicates that God knows that through His goodness He intends to put His King upon the throne, and He will do it in a robust and powerful manner.

What will take place here is a symbolic crowning, but it pictures the coming of Christ to this earth to reign, which is, of course, yet future.

Then take silver and gold, and make crowns, and set them upon the head of Joshua the son of Josedech, the high priest [Zech. 6:11].

This seems like a strange thing to do. Why did they place the crown on the head of Joshua the high priest rather than on the head of Zerubbabel who was in the line of David? The reason they were not to crown Zerubbabel is that God was not going to restore the line of David to the throne at that time. The fact of the matter is that the next one who will wear the crown of David will be the Lord Jesus Christ when He comes to this earth to establish His Kingdom. But crowning the high priest was very unusual because God kept the offices of king and priest entirely separate.

The explanation is found in the fact that Joshua, the high priest, in this passage is representative of the Lord Jesus Christ who is our great High Priest today. The Epistle to the Hebrews tells us to consider our great High Priest. Christ, after His resurrection, ascended into heaven, and as our great High Priest He has passed within the veil. He is seated now at God's right hand and is waiting for the time when His enemies will be made His footstool. He will come forth and establish His Kingdom here upon this earth. The chapter before us pictures His coronation.

Notice the sequence that is followed in this little Book of Zechariah. After the visions that depicted the judgment of God upon His people and upon all the gentile nations of the world, we have this, the coming of Christ and His crowning as the King of kings and Lord of lords.

It is interesting to see the threefold ministry of the Lord Jesus Christ in time spans. The first time span is His ministry as God's Prophet when he came to this earth over nineteen hundred years ago.

He came down here to *speak* for God, and He Himself was the *Word* of God as He revealed *God* in human form. And He revealed the *love* of God by dying upon the Cross for your sins and my sins. He was God's Prophet.

In the day in which you and I live He is God's *Priest.* When He ascended into heaven, He passed within the veil, and in the Holy of Holies He presented His own blood for our sins. Today He is there to make intercession for us. He intervenes for us when there is sin in our lives and we confess that sin to Him. He serves there as our High Priest.

One day in the future He will be coming out again. The Book of Revelation makes it very clear that He will come as King of kings and Lord of lords. Prophet, Priest, and King is the threefold ministry of Christ.

Now Christ is presented under another figure of speech—

> **And speak unto him, saying, Thus speaketh the LORD of hosts, saying, Behold the man whose name is The BRANCH; and he shall grow up out of his place, and he shall build the temple of the LORD [Zech. 6:12].**

"The BRANCH" is not the name of Joshua. It is a prophetic name which is given to the Lord Jesus Christ. He came to this earth over nineteen hundred years ago as the Branch, a root out of dry ground (see Isa. 53:2). The very fact that He came to humanity and came to a people at a time when they were subject to Rome is the most amazing thing in the world. He was called a root out of Jesse, the peasant, because by the time the Lord Jesus was born, the royal line of David had sunk back into poverty and obscurity. He was indeed the root out of a dry ground.

Suppose you were walking in a desert area—like the extremely desolate desert east of here in California. As you walk along you see no growing thing except a few cacti and a rattlesnake or two. Then suddenly you come upon a plant of iceberg lettuce growing there, luscious and green. You would be amazed. You would be unable to account for it. Well, the Lord Jesus was like that—a root out of a dry ground.

Jesus Christ is coming again as the Branch, and this time the Branch is going to rule the world.

"He shall grow up out of his place, and he shall build the temple of the LORD." You see, this is given as an encouragement to the remnant in their struggle to rebuild the temple. As we saw in the Book of Haggai, it looked small and insignificant to many of them, but in God's eyes His temple was one house. Although there is a series of temples— the wilderness tabernacle, Solomon's temple, Zerubbabel's temple, Herod's temple, the Great Tribulation temple, the millennial temple— God calls it one house. He didn't view Zerubbabel's temple as a separate house. Although it was considered unimportant by some of the people, God says that He is the one to judge its importance. And it is in His plan and purpose.

Many letters come to me with the lament, "I can't be very much for God." Well, that was also the cry of the discouraged remnant in Zechariah's day. The temple they were building seemed like nothing compared to the grandeur of Solomon's temple. But God was assuring them that the temple they were building was in His will and that He was the one to determine the importance of it.

Again let me say that I believe that some of the greatest pulpits we have in Southern California are not in churches; they happen to be sickbeds where some dear saint of God is confined. Recently I heard of a young man who listens to our Bible-teaching program. He is paralyzed from his neck down but is a radiant Christian and sends out Christian literature continually. I'm not sure but what his ministry for God is more important than mine or that of anyone which seems to be doing something great for God. We are to let God decide that. The important thing for you and me is to get into the will of God.

That was the point that Haggai and Zechariah were trying to get over to these people. They were encouraging them. They were saying, "You are doing what God wants you to do. Sure it looks small, but it is in the plan and purpose of God. That makes it great and big. It is going to eventuate in the coming of the Lord Jesus Christ to this earth to establish His Kingdom."

"Behold the man whose name is The BRANCH." The word of God speaks of the Lord Jesus Christ as "The Branch" in a fourfold way. (1) He is called the Branch of David: "Behold, the days come, saith the LORD, that I will raise unto David a righteous Branch, and a King shall reign and prosper, and shall execute judgment and justice in the earth" (Jer. 23:5). Here Christ is presented as the King, the Branch of David. (2) He is spoken of as Jehovah's *Servant*, the Branch; as we have already seen in chapter 3 verse 8: "Here now, O Joshua the high priest, thou, and thy fellows that sit before thee: for they are men wondered at: for, behold, I will bring forth my servant the BRANCH." (3) And here in chapter 6 verse 12 He is called "the *man* whose name is The BRANCH" (italics mine). (4) Finally, He is presented as the Branch of Jehovah: "In that day shall the branch of the LORD [Jehovah] be beautiful and glorious, and the fruit of the earth shall be excellent and comely for them that are escaped of Israel" (Isa. 4:2).

It is interesting that the Gospel records in the New Testament present the Lord Jesus in the same fourfold way. In the Gospel of Matthew He is the King, the Branch of David; in the Gospel of Mark He is Jehovah's *Servant*, the Branch; in the Gospel of Luke He is presented as the perfect *Man* whose name is the Branch; and in the Gospel of John He is the Branch of Jehovah, *God* the Son. This is a marvelous portrait that we have of Jesus as He was when He walked on this earth as a member of the human family.

> **Even he shall build the temple of the LORD; and he shall bear the glory, and shall sit and rule upon his throne; and he shall be a priest upon his throne: and the counsel of peace shall be between them both.**

> **And the crowns shall be to Helem, and to Tobijah, and to Jedaiah, and to Hen the son of Zephaniah, for a memorial in the temple of the LORD [Zech. 6:13–14].**

"Even he shall build the temple of the LORD." "Even he" is the sprout, the Branch who grew out of poverty and obscurity. "He shall build the temple of the LORD," refers to the millennial temple.

Christ the Messiah, "shall sit and rule upon his throne; and he shall be a priest upon his throne." He shall be both King and Priest. The two offices will be combined in one person.

"The crowns shall be . . . for a memorial in the temple of the LORD." Joshua did not wear these crowns. They were placed upon his head only for the symbolic crowning. Then, according to Jewish tradition, they were placed as symbols in the top windows of the temple for a memorial, serving as a reminder that the Messiah would come and that He would be not only the King but He also would be the Priest.

> **And they that are far off shall come and build in the temple of the LORD, and ye shall know that the LORD of hosts hath sent me unto you. And this shall come to pass, if ye will diligently obey the voice of the LORD your God [Zech. 6:15].**

"And they that are far off shall come and build in the temple of the LORD." Notice Merrill Unger's comments on this verse (p. 115):

> The deputation from far away Babylon bringing an offering of silver and gold for the temple, which was then in the process of construction, was the occasion for Zechariah's prediction of a future glorious temple to be established in Jerusalem as a House of Prayer for all nations, and to which even the Gentile peoples from afar shall flow, bringing their worship and their gifts.

Isaiah also speaks of the coming of gentile nations to the temple in Jerusalem during the Millennium: "And it shall come to pass in the last days, that the mountain of the LORD's house shall be established in the top of the mountains, and shall be exalted above the hills; and all nations shall flow unto it" (Isa. 2:2).

Let me remind you that back in verses 12 and 13 of this chapter it says that Christ (the Branch) shall build the temple of the Lord. And in the verse before us it says that "they that are far off shall come and build in the temple of the Lord." The nations shall build in the temple of the Lord in that they will bring their wealth into it. We need to make this distinction because only the Lord Jesus Himself will build the temple. Isaiah also says, "Also the sons of the stranger [Gentile], that join themselves to the LORD, to serve him, and to love the name of the LORD. . . . Even them will I bring to my holy mountain, and make them joyful in my house of prayer: their burnt offerings and their sacrifices shall be accepted upon mine altar; for mine house shall be called an house of prayer for all people" (Isa. 56:6–7).

"And ye shall know that the LORD of hosts hath sent me unto you." Apparently this means that Christ, the Messiah, will Himself establish the truth of God's Word.

"And this shall come to pass, if ye will diligently obey the voice of the LORD your God." I do not understand this to mean that the *fulfillment* of the prophecy will depend upon their obedience, because the prophecy is in the eternal plan and purpose of God. Rather, their *participation* in it depends upon their faith and obedience.

As we conclude the first major division of the Book of Zechariah, we need to locate it in the stream of history and prophecy. It is possible to lose our way through this section and, by so doing, miss one of the greatest lessons of Scripture and one of the greatest principles that God puts down in His Word. I urge those who attempt to teach prophecy to study this little book very carefully. It will deliver them from making some wild and weird interpretations.

Because the visions of Zechariah are highly symbolic, we are apt to come to the conclusion that they are just haphazard dream-stuff of a prophet of long ago. Folk who consider them totally unrelated to each other feel free to interpret them in any way they choose. There is a danger of lifting out one of the visions from its context and giving it an absurd interpretation. We must remember that one of the great rules of interpreting prophecy is that no prophecy is of any *private* interpretation—that is, it must be fitted into its proper place in the whole body of prophecy.

We need to keep in mind that all of the visions given to Zechariah are connected and related. They have meaning which is local and also they give an outline of history. They picture the whole future of the nation Israel, including the destruction of her enemies and her cleansing and restoration to her high priestly witness. The section finalizes with the coming of Christ to the earth as the great Priest-King to reign on the earth.

All of this was given by God through Zechariah as an encouragement to the discouraged remnant in his day who were struggling to build the temple. Not only was the work moving slowly and with difficulty, but it seemed so small and inconsequential compared to Solomon's temple and to the great heathen temples they had seen in Babylon and later in the Medo-Persian Empire. However, Israel was in a time of peace, and it was time for them to build.

Now I would like to call your attention to the threefold meaning. There is what is known as (1) the contemporary meaning, (2) the continuing meaning, and (3) the consummation of all things.

The contemporary meaning is that Zechariah was speaking into a local situation. He was addressing the people of his day regarding their problems. He was urging his own people not to be discouraged but to know that they are in the eternal plan and purpose of God. The little temple they were building would finally usher in the great millennial temple which the Messiah Himself would build.

The continuing meaning is a message for our day. You see, "All scripture is given by inspiration of God, and is profitable . . ." (2 Tim. 3:16). All of it has a message for us although not all of it was written to us. For instance, God has not asked us to build a temple. A few years ago many Christians tried to get stone out of Indiana and move it over to Israel to help them build the temple. That was a ridiculous idea. Our business is not to get the marble to Israel to help them build the temple; our business is to get to them the message of the One who is the Rock of Ages, the One who is the Stone cut out without hands (see Dan. 2:45), who said of Himself, "And whosoever shall fall on this stone shall be broken: but on whomsoever it shall fall, it will grind him to powder" (Matt. 21:44). If we don't fall upon Him, come in repentance to Him, in this age of grace, the day will come when we will have to bear His judgment. We have seen that God judges nations—the Babylonian, Medo-Persian, and Graeco-Macedonian Empires have come and gone. My friend, are you blind to the fact that God is moving today in the history of this world? Do you realize that

God is judging our own nation? Vietnam was a place of shame and humiliation. What did we actually accomplish over there? The billions of dollars spent on war costs should have been invested years earlier in Bibles and missionaries.

Current events should certainly teach us how quickly God can raise up a nation and how quickly He can bring it down. America rose to be the strongest nation on the earth, but we stumbled along in our sin and in our arrogance. Fifty years ago absolutely no one would have believed that the United States would yield to the demands of a few desert sheiks who ruled over a few people and some mangy camels. No one would have seen the relationship between the camel and a Cadillac. Yet today we see the wealth of the world going into Arabian oil. They will bankrupt our nation; yet we close our eyes to what is going on. God can raise nations and bring down nations in whatever way He chooses.

If you listen to the news media, you will become discouraged. Besides that, you'll get brainwashed. If you look at Washington, D.C., you will feel like giving up—or throwing up! I don't know about you, but I am tired of hearing panel discussions by politicians, educators, the military, athletes, and the movie colony. I don't think that any of them have a message for us right now. Perhaps you can hear the still small voice of God in the visions of Zechariah. His visions are not weird and wild, and no weird and wild interpretation is satisfactory. They teach us that God's purpose will prevail and that God is moving in history to accomplish His purpose.

The final of the threefold meanings is the *consummation* of all things. History is flowing in the channel of prophecy. Again let me repeat verse 12: "Thus speaketh the LORD of hosts, saying, Behold the man whose name is The BRANCH; and he shall grow up out of his place, and he shall build the temple of the LORD." The Branch, as we have seen, is none other than the Lord Jesus Christ, a root out of dry ground, who died on a cross for us. But He is coming again to reign. "In that day shall the branch of the LORD be beautiful and glorious, and the fruit of the earth shall be excellent and comely for them that are escaped of Israel" (Isa. 4:2). He shall be the *priest* upon His throne.

Knowing this should help us to keep things in perspective. There may be some little group of believers who meet on a back street, but they are meeting in the name of Christ and they are seeking to honor Him. They are studying His Word, and they really want to do His will. They sing with sincerity,

> My Jesus, I love Thee, I know Thou art mine,
> For Thee all the follies of sin I resign;
> My gracious Redeemer, my Savior art Thou;
> If ever I loved Thee, my Jesus, 'tis now.
> —William R. Featherstone

That little group may be unknown to the world, but it is more important in the plan and program of God than the meetings held by heads of state in the capitals of the world. This is hard for many folk to believe because the world does not see things from God's point of view.

You see, that little group of believers will join in with a mighty chorus in heaven some day, singing to the Lamb: ". . . Thou art worthy to take the book, and to open the seals thereof: for thou wast slain, and hast redeemed us to God by thy blood out of every kindred, and tongue, and people, and nation; and hast made us unto our God kings and priests: and we shall reign on the earth" (Rev. 5:9–10). That is the goal toward which we are moving. The world may ignore these believers and multitudes simply pass them by; yet they are important in the plan and purpose of God.

This section of Zechariah should help us see things from God's perspective. This tremendous passage of Scripture still has a message for you and me today.

CHAPTER 7

THEME: Historic interlude; question concerning a religious ritual (fasting); threefold answer; when the heart is right, the ritual is right; when the heart is wrong, the ritual is wrong

HISTORIC INTERLUDE

In chapters 7 and 8 we have what I have labeled a historic interlude. It is very similar to what we also have in the little prophecy of Haggai. In the middle of that prophecy, Haggai was sent to the priest to ask concerning a law: When anything that is ceremonially clean touches that which is unclean, will it make it clean? And, of course, the answer is that it will not. And when that which is ceremonially unclean touches that which is clean, will it make it unclean? The answer is yes, it will. In this historic interlude here in Zechariah, we have the same problem approached from a little different angle.

QUESTION CONCERNING A RITUAL (FASTING)

And it came to pass in the fourth year of king Darius, that the word of the LORD came unto Zechariah in the fourth day of the ninth month, even in Chisleu [Zech. 7:1].

The impressive thing here is that again Zechariah is going to have a message for these people, and it is a very important message. He makes it clear that it is not his own message, but it is "the word of the LORD."

"In the fourth year of king Darius . . . in the fourth day of the ninth month, even in Chisleu." If you want me to put this in terms of our calendar, it was December 4, 518 B.C. This is the same period in which Haggai was speaking to the people in a very practical way.

> When they had sent unto the house of God Sherezer and
> Regemmelech, and their men, to pray before the Lord
> [Zech. 7:2].

David Baron's comment (p. 210) will help us better understand this
verse:

> It will be noticed that, together with the Revised Version, and
> almost all modern scholars, we discard the rendering given of
> the first line of the 2nd verse in the Authorized Version,
> namely, "When they sent unto the House of God." Now, Beth-el
> does mean literally "House of God"; but it is never used of the
> Temple, but only and always of the well-known town of
> Ephraim, one of the great centers of the Israelitish idolatrous
> worship set up by Jeroboam the son of Nebat.

In other words, what we have here is a delegation of men sent from
Bethel, which means "house of God." It was called the house of God
by Jacob at that time in his life when he thought he was running away
from God as well as from his father and his brother Esau. He spent the
night at this place, and God gave him a vision. Jacob said of Bethel,
". . . this is none other but the house of God, and this is the gate of
heaven" (Gen. 28:17).

Bethel was located in the northern kingdom of Israel and is the
place where Jeroboam put one of the golden calves to be worshiped.
This delegation was not made up of men of the tribe of Judah. They
were probably of the tribe of Ephraim. The fact that this delegation
came down from Bethel indicates that people from the ten so-called
"lost-tribes" were not lost at all—some of them were living at Bethel.
If you will read the Book of Ezra very carefully, you will find that
many people who returned from the Babylonian captivity returned to
towns that were actually north of the Sea of Galilee, an area that belonged to the ten tribes which constituted the northern kingdom of
Israel. All twelve tribes were represented in those who returned, although very few actually returned, less than 60,000 all told.

My friend, there are no "ten lost tribes of Israel." Those who returned from the Captivity naturally went back to the places from

which they had come, and many of them went to the northern part which was the kingdom of Israel. They happened to be folk born in the Babylonian captivity (Sherezer and Regemmelech are Babylonian names) who returned as Jews back to their own tribe. If you feel that Anglo-Saxons or any other gentile race makes up the "ten lost tribes," may I say to you, you are very much lost in the maze of Scripture. You may be lost, but the ten tribes are not lost.

> And to speak unto the priests which were in the house of the LORD of hosts, and to the prophets, saying, Should I weep in the fifth month, separating myself, as I have done these so many years? [Zech. 7:3].

These men have come down from Bethel to speak to the priests in the temple at Jerusalem, and they have come with a question. The question has to do with a ritual: Is a ritual right or is a ritual wrong? The people had begun to fast before the Babylonian captivity and had continued to do so during the Captivity. Psalm 137:1–2 says, "By the rivers of Babylon, there we sat down, yea, we wept, when we remembered Zion. We hanged our harps upon the willows in the midst thereof." They just sobbed out their souls there, and that became a religious function. Actually, God had never given them fast days; He gave seven *feast* days. It was their own idea to fast. They had set aside days of fasting and days of weeping and mourning during their captivity, and they continued it after the Captivity, but God was not blessing them. A certain amount of prosperity had come; many of them were building their homes and were getting very comfortable, even affluent. Yet they were weeping and mourning, and they said, "We've been doing this but God hasn't blessed us." The question here is of the right and wrong of a ritual.

This is an important question for us because we are seeing today a recrudescence of ritualistic religion. There is a movement toward formalism, toward adopting a ritual. Formalism is always in evidence when people cease to think. When people get away from the person of Christ, they start either getting up and down or marching around—they have to start doing something. This indicates a time of spiritual

decline. There was a time when people fought over the prayer book in
Europe, as if that were important—whether you should stand up or sit
down or kneel or just how you should pray. There are many people
who want a liturgy or an elaborate ritual. There are religions that are
called Christian religions that are ritualistic or liturgical. Even we
nonconformists who have come out of the Reformation say that a ritual
is repugnant, we despise it, we see in it evil continually, but our services have a certain amount of ritual. We open with the doxology, and
everyone stands up for that. We close with a benediction, and somewhere in between there is an offering and a sermon.

God gave to the nation Israel a religion—it is the only religion He
ever gave—and it was ritualistic. Is a ritual right or is a ritual
wrong?—that is the question of these people. They say, "We've been
fasting and weeping and wailing, and it looks pretty silly now. It's
gotten very boring. After all, it is a religious rite we are going through,
and we're not getting any results. God doesn't seem to be blessing us.
Should we keep on doing this?"

THREEFOLD ANSWER

Zechariah will give the people God's answer concerning this question. God doesn't come out and say that it is wrong to fast, nor does He
say it is right. He doesn't answer the question directly, and yet He
answers the question. We will find that there is actually a threefold
answer to this question concerning a religious ritual. The first answer
is that when the heart is right, the ritual is right (vv. 4–7). The second
answer is that when the heart is wrong, the ritual is wrong (vv. 8–14).
The third answer is found in chapter 8: God's purpose concerning
Jerusalem is unchanged by any ritual. That will answer a great many
folk today who are saying, "Let's do this or that to hasten the coming
of Christ." My friend, you cannot move it up one second by anything
you do. Don't you know that He is running this universe? Anything
that you do is not going to interfere with His plan or program. These
people thought that a ritual might have something to do with chang-
ing God's plan. In chapter 8 God will let them know that He intends to
accomplish His purpose.

WHEN THE HEART IS RIGHT, THE RITUAL IS RIGHT

Then came the word of the LORD of hosts unto me, saying,

Speak unto all the people of the land, and to the priests, saying, When ye fasted and mourned in the fifth and seventh month, even those seventy years, did ye at all fast unto me, even to me? [Zech. 7:4–5].

"When ye fasted and mourned in the fifth and seventh month"—that would be the months of August and October. "Even those seventy years"—that is, while Israel was in captivity.

"Did ye at all fast unto me, even to me?" God says to them, "When you went through your ritual, did you do it for Me? Did you do it to honor Me and to praise Me? Or did you do it as a legalistic sort of exercise that would build up something on the credit side which would make you acceptable to Me and cause Me to bless you?" God does not approve nor does He condemn the ritual. He inquires into their motive.

The people say that they have been fasting "these so many years." Oh boy, you can read between the lines there! Worshiping God had really become boring to them. And the Lord is saying to them, "If you really want to know the truth, I was bored with you also. I thought you were very boring." I think there are a lot of so-called Christian services which cause God to yawn. I think that He says, "Ho hum, there they go again, jumping through some little hoop as though they think that it will please Me."

And when ye did eat, and when ye did drink, did not ye eat for yourselves, and drink for yourselves? [Zech. 7:6].

God says, "You didn't fast unto Me, and when the fasting was over, you couldn't wait to get to the table. And when you were eating, did you do it unto Me?" Paul wrote to the Corinthians, "But meat commendeth us not to God: for neither, if we eat, are we the better; neither, if we eat not, are we the worse" (1 Cor. 8:8). He went on to say later, "Whether therefore ye eat, or drink, or whatsoever ye do, do all to the glory of God" (1 Cor. 10:31). If you can fast to the glory of God, go ahead and fast, but if you are doing it for some reason other than that high motive, don't do it. Our Christian faith is not a Sunday affair. The test of the Sunday service is the life that is lived the next day. In the last part of this chapter, God is going to deal with Israel on the very specifics of their business dealings, their social contacts, and their amusements. These were the things that revealed that they did not live their lives unto the Lord at all. There is something more important than the ritual which will determine whether the ritual is right or not.

> Should ye not hear the words which the LORD hath cried by the former prophets, when Jerusalem was inhabited and in prosperity, and the cities thereof round about her, when men inhabited the south and the plain? [Zech. 7:7].

"The south [the Negeb] and the plain." That section all the way up from Beer-sheba, whether you go to Hebron or over to the coast toward Ekron, looks like a big pasture land. It reminds me of the plains of West Texas where I lived as a boy in the days before they irrigated that land. When a wind would come through, it could really blow up a sandstorm the likes of which you had never seen or heard of before. The plains around Beer-sheba are the same kind of land. God says to the people here, "You went through all these rituals before when you were in the land, and what happened? You went into captivity because you did not obey Me, you did not listen to the voice of My prophets."

WHEN THE HEART IS WRONG, THE RITUAL IS WRONG

Beginning with verse 8, God is going to show that a ritual is wrong if the heart is wrong. This is not another way of saying the same thing as He has just said. God will put down on the people's lives specific commandments, the commandments that have to do with a man's relationship to man as well as to God, and it will show that their hearts were not right. My friend, it is wrong to think that we can serve Christ and go through a little ritual of doing something while we are not really right with Him. What the Lord Jesus said to Simon Peter following His resurrection is truly beautiful. Do you know what I would have done if I had been in the Lord's place and had come to Simon Peter? I would have bawled him out for denying me. I would have told him what kind of fellow I thought he was. But the Lord Jesus said to him, "Do you love Me?" My friend, it is not the ritual you go through, but it is the attitude of your heart that is important to Him.

To some church members, religion is a rite or a ritual or a legalistic and lifeless form, a liturgical system marked by meaningless and wearisome verbiage. There is a lot of religious garbage in our so-called conservative and evangelical churches also. There is a ceaseless quoting of tired adjectives and a jumble of pious platitudes. We so often hear people say, "We want to share our faith." My friend, most people don't have enough faith to share. It's not your faith when you share about how wonderful you are or what wonderful things God did for you. You are to witness to Jesus Christ, who He is and what He did for you. In talking about salvation, people say, "Commit your life to Him." If you ask them what they mean, they say, "Yield your life to Him." Do you really think He wants your life? He says that our righteousness and even our so-called good deeds are filthy rags in His sight. God doesn't want your dirty laundry, my friend. I am afraid that we have gotten into the habit of using words that take away the real meaning of the gospel. There is another word that is surely being worn out and whose tread is really becoming thin. Love is a high word of Scripture, but it has been worn out on the freeway of present-day usage. It has been emasculated of its rich, vital, virile, and vigorous Bible meaning. It's been degraded to the level of a bumper sticker which says, "Honk if you love Jesus!" The other day I noticed that the people ahead of me were honking and going around a little car that was being driven very slowly in the fast lane of the freeway. Car after car had to detour around this man. As I came up to him, I thought that I would honk at him also, but then I saw his bumper sticker which said, "Honk if you love Jesus!" As I went around him, I gave him a hard look. If I could have had an opportunity to speak to him, I would have told him that if you love Jesus, you don't run around honking your horn. If you love Jesus you're going to live a life of obedience to Him, and you will be courteous to other people.

My point is that today there is a great deal of "churchianity" that is bland and bloodless, tasteless and colorless. It is devoid of warmth and feeling. There is no personal relationship with Christ that is meaningful and productive. One liberal pastor wrote that it made him sick to hear people talk of a personal relationship with Christ. I would surely make him sick if he would listen to me because the thing you have to have, my friend, is a personal relationship with Christ. Your ritual and your liturgy are not worth the snap of your fingers unless you have a life that is related to Jesus Christ.

If there is no deep yearning for a life that is well pleasing to Him, if there is no stimulating desire to know Him and His Word, church membership is just like a young man falling in love with a furnished apartment and marrying an electric stove, a refrigerator, a vacuum cleaner, a garbage disposal, and a wet mop! That is just about all it amounts to. A maiden lady was asked why she had never gotten married, and she gave a very interesting answer. "I have a stove that smokes, I have a dog that growls around the house, I have a parrot that cusses, and I have a lazy cat that loafs around all day and then is out half the night—so why do I need a husband?" May I say to you, that is the kind of relationship that a great many folk have to God and to Christ. Let's stop playing church today and start loving Christ and living for Him!

I want to share with you two of the most remarkable letters that I have received in many a day. The first comes from a little town in Tennessee:

> I discovered your program out of Memphis only about six months ago, just when I needed it most. Isn't that just like our lovely Lord? I am a born-again Christian, only two years old. That is truly something for a 55-year-old grandmother to have to admit. My husband is a retired regular army dentist—a heart

patient. We moved 33 times in 26 years before retiring on this little farm here in the boondocks. We played church. I even taught a women's Sunday school class, and my husband was a deacon. I can't speak for him, but all I had was head knowledge and very little heart knowledge. The young minister in the church where we have gone for 14 years is so liberal he thinks the belief in the virgin birth unnecessary and sees no conflict between transcendental meditation and Christianity. We stuck it out for a year and then left the church. I would be less than honest to say I don't miss a church home since I've had church homes like that.

The other letter comes from Southern California:

I am a wife and mother under 30, and I've been a Christian since I was 3½. I have often thought of writing but didn't think I had anything meaningful to say. Well, I've changed my mind. Several years ago I knew a lady quite well who was constantly pushing your program at me. This lady was a terrible housekeeper, had an unhappy husband and marriage and five unruly children. But she listened to her Christian programs from morning till night. Naturally, I associated her fanaticism with you and would not listen. During the past three years, however, I have been listening to you weekdays and sometimes on Sunday before church . . . I love the study of the Word. I get so much from your theology and your knowledge of the Scriptures. I wish that I could find a pastor locally who preached as well. Our time is so short, and I'm glad you're filling each minute with vital news of God. I wish I could have seen past that lady's disorderly life a long time ago. God bless you in your work, thou good and faithful servant.

Here was a woman who listened to all the Christian programs, who was a fanatical Christian, but who had a home and a life that were a disgrace to the cause of Christ. My friend, a ritual is no good to a person like that. Likewise, there's nothing wrong with a ritual if you are right with God and if you love Jesus Christ.

This reminds me of the little girl and the story of the three bears. The little girl's mother was having guests for dinner and she sent the little girl upstairs to go to bed early. She gave her instructions, telling her she knew how to undress, put on her pajamas, and kneel down to have her prayer. The next morning at the breakfast table, the mother asked the little girl how she did. "Just fine" was the reply.

"Did you say your prayers?"

"Well, kind of."

"What do you mean 'kind of'?" the mother asked.

The little girl explained, "Well, I got down on my knees to say that prayer I always say, and I just thought that maybe God got tired of hearing the same thing all the time, so I just crawled into bed, and I told Him the story of the three little bears."

I think God enjoyed that evening when that precious little girl already sensed that there is something wrong with a ritual when the heart is not in it. I think God listened to the story of the three bears. I wish that some church services today could be that interesting, and I think it would get God's attention. Why do we have all these problem churches today? Why do we have all these problem Christians today? It is because we are going through a rite, we are going through a ritual, we are performing a liturgy without a heart for God Himself. Even we in fundamental churches open with the doxology, close with a benediction, with something in between, and we feel like we've been to church. Have we really? Have we been drawn to the person of Christ? Do we know Him? Do we love Him? You can go through any ritual you want to, and it will be all right if you are right with the Lord, my friend.

The importance of ritual is still a very moot question for people today. Should I go through this ceremony or should I do this or should I do that? I believe that certain ceremonies, certain rituals are important. I believe there are two sacraments in the church, and I believe they are all-important. One sacrament is baptism, and the other is the Lord's Supper. The important thing is that baptism is believer's baptism. The emphasis should be taken off the mode and put on the heart of the one being baptized: Is he born again? I personally believe in immersion although I was raised in a church that taught otherwise. I have been both sprinkled and immersed—that way I can't miss, as you can see. My wife was Southern Baptist, she was immersed, and she still thinks that was pretty important. I like to kid her, "It will sure be embarrassing for you if you and I get to heaven and find that immersion was not the right mode. I've had the other, and you haven't." I say that facetiously, and I say it for this reason: As important as the sacraments are, they are no good, my friend, unless you've turned to Jesus Christ and you have a personal relationship with Him and your sins have been forgiven. I am also afraid that the Lord's Supper is absolutely meaningless for many people—it would be better for them if they didn't go through with it. But if your heart is right, the Lord's Supper is absolutely important. It was Lange who made this statement: "God's eye of grace and our eye of faith meet in the sacraments."

Before the Captivity, God judged Jerusalem when the hearts of the people were far from Him although they were going through the rituals. In verse 7 God said to them, "Should ye not hear the words which the LORD hath cried by the former prophets, when Jerusalem was inhabited and in prosperity, and the cities thereof round about her, when men inhabited the south and the plain?" In effect He said, "You went through the rituals before the Captivity, and I sent you into captivity. Why? The ritual had nothing to do with it. It was because your hearts were wrong, and the heart is the thing that is important."

In the last section of this chapter, God very specifically spells out those things the people were doing which alienated them from Himself. He will be dealing with that part of the Ten Commandments which have to do with man's relationship to man. The previous section of the chapter had to do with a man's relationship to God—when the heart is not rightly related to God, the ritual is wrong. In this section the ritual is wrong if the heart is wrong. By putting these commandments right down upon their lives, God will specifically reveal the things they were doing wrong.

We are not dealing with sin today as we should. If you knew me like I know myself, you would not continue to read what I have to say. But wait a minute, if I knew you like you know yourself, I don't think I'd bother to write to you. May I say to you, we are sinners. When I was a pastor in downtown Los Angeles, I knew a dear little lady who had been a Bible teacher. Whenever I would talk about the fact that we are saved sinners, she always wanted to correct me. She would say, "Dr. McGee, after we are saved, we're not sinners."

"I don't know about you, but I'm still a sinner," I would tell her.

"If your sins have been forgiven, you're not a sinner."

"No, I'm a saved sinner, I'm a forgiven sinner, but I'm still a sinner, and I will be a sinner as long as I live on this earth. 'Beloved, now are we the sons of God, and it doth not yet appear what we shall be: but we know that, when he shall appear, we shall be like him; for we shall see him as he is' (1 John 3:2). In that day when you see Vernon McGee, I won't be a sinner, but until that day, I'm a sinner."

My friend, both you and I are sinners. All of us are sinners before God, and I am delighted to know that this belief is coming back into style. I have a clipping of a prominent doctor of psychology who states that he used to go along with Freudian psychology which teaches that the reason you are such a lousy person is because your mama didn't give you the proper affection that you should have had or that maybe you weren't a breast-fed baby and that is the reason you have gone in for promiscuous sex. My friend, what nonsense that is! Now this doctor has changed his position, and he writes, "The realities of personal guilt and sin have been glossed over as only symptoms of emotional illness or environmental conditioning for which the individual isn't considered responsible. But there is sin which cannot be subsumed under verbal artifacts such as disease, delinquency, deviancy. There is immorality. There is unethical behavior. There is wrongdoing." In other words, my friend, you and I are sinners. I have been saying that for years. Even when I studied psychology in college, I did not buy behaviorism. I frankly believe that God alone knows about humanity and about our hearts. "The heart is deceitful above all things, and desperately wicked: who can know it?" (Jer. 17:9). Only God knows it, and He alone knows it.

If we could see ourselves as God sees us, we couldn't stand ourselves. Only God could put up with us. Oh, if we would just come to the Word of God and rest in the Word of God! God is going to be specific with them and put these commandments right down upon their lives. This is what we need to do also. I do not mean to step on your toes, but I am trying to tell you what the Word of God says. Let me illustrate my point. If all the church officers in this country would simply read the Pastoral Epistles (1 and 2 Timothy and Titus) to see what are God's requirements for being an officer in the church, and if they would simply follow those requirements, over one-half of the church officers in this country would resign before next Sunday. The church would be better off, and I think a revival would break out in many places. When I teach those epistles, I receive less mail from my listeners than during any other period of time. Why? Because they do not like to hear what the Word of God has to say. Even some of us preachers would have to walk out of the pulpit and never enter it again if we really followed what the Word of God says.

There is little wonder that the church has the problem that it has. There is little wonder that it is filled with a bunch of babies, sucking their thumbs, crying loud and long unless they are given some attention, a rattle to play with, or maybe a yo-yo. They take some little course of instruction and think that that makes them a full-grown child of God in a few weeks. These little courses are not even an all-day sucker for the babe. During the Second World War when there was a shortage of officers, they instituted a ninety-day course to produce second lieutenants. They were called "the wonder boys." We sure have a lot of "wonder Christians" who know nothing about the Word of God.

Again let me illustrate what I am talking about. Although I have taken as long as five years to teach the entire Bible, I feel like I am a babe as far as the Word of God is concerned. I've missed so much even teaching at that slow pace. I hesitate to teach the Book of Revelation, although I consider it the most mechanical, the most simple book in the Word of God. I approach it with fear and trembling. Yet there are pastors and teachers who have been in a church or with a group for just a short period of time who are already teaching Revelation. My friend, there are sixty-five books that come before Revelation, but prophecy is popular and made to be sensational. Sir Robert Anderson calls this "the wild utterances of prophecy mongers." Many of us are willing to settle for the better things of life when God wants us to have the best things. Oh, that we would put our lives under the spotlight of the Word of God.

And the word of the LORD came unto Zechariah, saying [Zech. 7:8].

Zechariah isn't just giving his opinion. He is saying to the people, "This is what God has to say, and this is God's answer to you. The ritual is wrong if the heart is wrong."

Now God is going to put the spotlight down on the people—

Thus speaketh the LORD of hosts, saying, Execute true judgment, and shew mercy and compassions every man to his brother.

And oppress not the widow, nor the fatherless, the stranger, nor the poor; and let none of you imagine evil against his brother in your heart [Zech. 7:9–10].

It will be helpful for us to take a close look at the last of the Ten Commandments. The first four commandments have to do with a man's relationship to God. The next commandment is a bridge and has to do with man's relationship to his parents. There is a period in his life when that little fellow in the home looks up to his mama and papa; they are actually God to him, and that is the way God intended it to be. The reason children are to obey their parents when they're growing up is so that later on they will be able to obey the Lord Jesus. Now notice the last five commandments: "Thou shalt not kill. Thou shalt not commit adultery. Thou shalt not steal. Thou shalt not bear false witness against thy neighbour. Thou shalt not covet thy neighbour's house, thou shalt not covet thy neighbour's wife, nor his manservant, nor his maidservant, nor his ox, nor his ass, nor any thing that is thy neighbour's" (Exod. 20:13–17). You are not to covet his Cadillac nor the lovely home that he lives in—you are not to covet these things at all.

Notice how we can put these commandments right down upon our lives. "Thus, speaketh the LORD of hosts, saying, Execute true judgment"—don't bear false witness. "And shew mercy and compassions every man to his brother"—you are not to steal, not to lie, not to covet. "And oppress not the widow, nor the fatherless, the stranger, nor the poor"—oh, boy, this is getting right down where we live. "Let none of you imagine evil against his brother in your heart." The Lord Jesus brought all the commandments up to a higher plane, although He only cited two commandments as illustrations. But He said that if you are angry with your brother, you are guilty of murder.

God is saying that although Israel went through the rituals, you ought to have met them on Sunday, Monday, Tuesday, Wednesday, Thursday, and Friday! On Friday night they started through the rituals again, and they would weep and mourn and fast and bring sacrifices. In the Book of Malachi God says to them, "You say that those sacrifices made you sick. You ought to have been in My position—they *nauseated* Me."

> **But they refused to hearken, and pulled away the shoulder, and stopped their ears, that they should not hear [Zech. 7:11].**

The people did not want to hear what God wanted them to hear, and there are people today in the same position.

They "pulled away the shoulder"—how vivid this is! When I was a little fellow in southern Oklahoma, the little country school put on a program. I think I was in about the fifth grade, and my class was sitting down front. I was causing some kind of disturbance (I don't know why—I was such a good boy!) and my father, who was sitting in the back, walked down and touched me on the shoulder. I turned and pulled that shoulder away. Oh, what a brat I was to do a thing like that! My dad took me by the hand, led me out the side door, and he said, "Son, I'm going to give you a whipping." That wasn't anything new, but he went on to say, "I'm not going to give it to you because you were making a disturbance. I'm going to give it to you because you pulled away from me when I put my hand on your shoulder. You were disobedient." Then for the next few minutes he impressed upon me that I wasn't to do that sort of thing.

God says of Israel, "I touched them on the shoulder, and they pulled away the shoulder." There are many people in our churches today whom God is touching on the shoulder and saying, "Wait a minute. Don't do that. Don't live that kind of life." They pull away their shoulder, they stop their ears, and they don't want to hear what God has to say.

I was baby-sitting my little grandson out in the yard when he did something he shouldn't have done. He got into my flower bed and was ruining one of my camellias. I told him to get out, but he looked at me and said, "I'm not going to get out." (He takes after his grandmother quite a bit, as you can see!) He started back in, and I put my hand on his shoulder to stop him. He did that same thing—he pulled away. It reminded me of another little boy about sixty-five years ago. I knew what my dad had done, and since I'm his grandfather, I took him and turned him across my knee, and I gave him quite a little lesson. My daughter applauded me for it and said, "I thought you had him so spoiled that you'd never correct him."

"But they refused to hearken, and pulled away the shoulder, and stopped their ears, that they should not hear." This is what these spoiled brats who had come down from Bethel had been doing; in fact, the whole nation had been doing it. The reason Israel had gone into captivity was not because they didn't have light. God had put His hand on their shoulder, the prophets had spoken to them, but they "stopped their ears, that they should not hear." In other words, they turned their backs on God. They had broken the commandments which relate to God, and they were guilty before Him.

Going through a religious ritual will not do you a bit of good if your heart is not right, my friend. Until you get your life straightened out, there is no use becoming religious. Actually, that will only make you a member of the crowd the Lord Jesus called hypocrites. Have you ever noticed that He never called a believer a hypocrite? In the Bible, you'll never find a real believer called a hypocrite. It is those who pretend, those who have religion, those who have, as the Lord Jesus said, washed the outside of the cup while the inside is still putrid, who are called hypocrites (see Matt. 23:25–26). This was the problem with the people of Israel. God simply put down on their lives the Ten Commandments, beginning with the commandments which relate to man. How were they acting in their business and social and home lives? When He did this, it really showed them up, and it showed the reason why God had not heard and answered their prayers.

> Yea, they made their hearts as an adamant stone, lest they should hear the law, and the words which the LORD of hosts hath sent in his spirit by the former prophets: therefore came a great wrath from the LORD of hosts [Zech. 7:12].

"Therefore came a great wrath from the LORD of hosts." The destruction of Jerusalem by Nebuchadnezzar and the carrying away of these people into Babylon was a sad thing, a tragic thing, an awful thing. They were religious, they were going through a ritual, but their hearts were far from God, and they were a disgrace to Him.

> Therefore it is come to pass, that as he cried, and they would not hear; so they cried, and I would not hear, saith the LORD of hosts [Zech. 7:13].

God says to these people, "I cried to you, and I pled with you, but you would not listen to Me." Then when they got into trouble, they said, "We don't want to go into captivity. We'll come back to You." And God now says, "I didn't hear you." There are a lot of prayers today that God doesn't hear. I get a little weary of this sentimental rot that is shown on our television screens. In these weepy sob stories, some reprobate—either man or woman—lives any kind of life he wants, but when his little child gets sick, he goes in and kneels by the bed to plead with God for the life of the child! I don't think God hears that prayer, my friend. I'll be honest with you: you've got to get right with God yourself before you are going to get anywhere with Him by praying. God makes it clear that the other is nothing in the world but religious rot, and it will not get you anywhere at all.

But I scattered them with a whirlwind among all the
nations whom they knew not. Thus the land was desolate after them, that no man passed through nor returned: for they laid the pleasant land desolate [Zech.
7:14].

I want you to note that God says that He made the pleasant land desolate. He not only judged the people but also the land. Many people go
to that land today and are greatly disappointed because they've heard
that it is the land of milk and honey. It was that at one time; it was like
the Garden of Eden. But I think people are trying to kid themselves
when they say today, "Oh, isn't this a beautiful land!" My friend, it is
rocky, it is dry, it is a most desolate place. If you can find anything
pretty on the way down from Jerusalem to Jericho and the Dead Sea, I
wish that you would point it out to me. It is as bad as the desert in
eastern California and in Arizona. It is really a desolate place, and
there are very few beautiful spots in that land. It *was* the pleasant
land, but it's the desolate land today.

One of the proofs that prophecy is not being fulfilled today is the
fact that the land has not been restored. I know that the Jews have
moved back there and have become a nation, but they have been in
trouble ever since. At the time I am writing this, I have just heard from
a friend who has recently returned from there. He tells me that taxes in
Israel are higher than in any place in the world. Are you going to call
that "the promised land," and are you going to hold God responsible
for that? I don't think He has returned the people back to that land at
the present time. My friend also reported to me that a great many of
the people who are there now want to leave the land. What is that
going to do to these Bible teachers who are trying to date everything in
prophecy from the beginning of the modern nation of Israel? My
friend, Israel is still a desolate land today, but it's going to become the
pleasant land again someday.

CHAPTER 8

THEME: God's purpose concerning Jerusalem unchanged by any ritual

Chapter 8 is God's third explanation to the people concerning their question: We have gone through the ritual and the liturgy—why hasn't God blessed us? His first answer was that, when the heart is right, the ritual is all right. His second answer was that, when the heart is wrong, the ritual is wrong. In other words, the ritual doesn't have anything to do with it; it is the heart that is important. Some expositors call chapter 8 the positive answer to this question, with chapter 7 being the negative aspect of the answer. I want to say to you, the answer in chapter 8 is positively positive: God's purpose concerning Jerusalem is unchanged by any ritual. Whether you go through a ritual or you don't go through it, you are not going to change God's plan and purpose. Thank God for that. Thank God that He will carry through His plan and His purpose.

Five words occur in this chapter which are very important. In fact, you can hang the meaning of this chapter on these words.

1. First is the expression, "Lord of hosts." Dr. Merrill Unger gives the interpretation of this expression as "Lord of armies," and that probably is a more literal translation. "The Lord of hosts" or "the Lord of armies" occurs eighteen times in this chapter. Apparently, He is very important in this chapter—"the Lord of hosts."

2. *Jerusalem* occurs six times, and *Zion* occurs twice. Jerusalem is a geographical city located in Israel, over in the Middle East today. It never has changed; it is still the same place. When God says Jerusalem, He means Jerusalem. He does not mean London or Washington, D.C., or Rome or Los Angeles or any other place. When He says Jerusalem, God means Jerusalem.

3. The word *jealous* occurs three times.

4. The word *remnant* occurs twice. Remember that it was only a remnant from all twelve tribes that returned to the land—they did not

return from only the two southern tribes. There were very few, even from Judah, who came back. Approximately sixty thousand returned to that land.

5. The final expression, "Thus saith the LORD," occurs ten times. When God keeps repeating that, do you know what it means? It means "thus saith the LORD"—not Vernon McGee, not any man, but it is God who is saying this. I do not speak or write in order to be popular today. I would change my tactics quite a bit if I wanted to do that. I'm attempting to teach the Word of God, and if your toes get stepped on, God is the one who is stepping on them. I'm simply reading what the Word of God has to say. The reason that a book like Zechariah is not being taught today is that people do not like to have their toes stepped on. Yet I am thankful for and amazed at the number of people who are hearing the Word of God. It's a glorious day in which to live, unlike the day in which I began my ministry.

Some commentators feel that chapter 8 puts the Ten Commandments down on the people of Israel even more than chapter 7 did. I do not feel that that is accurate. My feeling is that the last part of chapter 7 put the Ten Commandments down on them, and they were weighed in the balances and were found wanting—they did not measure up to God's standard at all. Then in chapter 8, especially in the first eight verses, we find that God's ultimate purpose is not changed concerning His people—the nation Israel, the land, and Jerusalem. At the present moment, God is not fulfilling any prophecy concerning Israel. He is dealing today with the church; He is calling out a body of believers in the church. And the church and Israel are entirely two separate entities. When God will get through calling out the church, I do not know. It's not geared to any man's calendar at all. It's on God's calendar, but He has never let any of us see it. God's Word doesn't tell us when He will take the church out of this earth, but when He does, He will turn to the people of Israel again. These prophecies here in chapter 8 are simply saying that their return to the land in Zechariah's day was very small but that it is an adumbration, a little miniature picture, of a return to the land that is coming in the future.

Again the word of the LORD of hosts came to me, saying,

> Thus saith the LORD of hosts; I was jealous for Zion with
> great jealousy, and I was jealous for her with great fury
> [Zech. 8:1-2].

When God says that He is jealous, it is not the same as man's jealousy, but He does have the same thing in mind. I feel sorry for any woman who makes the statement, "My husband is not jealous of me." If it is true, it means that her husband does not love her. I don't know about you, but I'm jealous of my wife. I married her for myself because I love her. I don't intend to share her with anybody else, and I will not—that's for sure. I'm jealous of her. God says that concerning Israel, and He says it to the church today. If you think that you can live for the world and the flesh and the Devil and then serve God on Sunday, you are wrong. You won't make it, my friend. If you are His child and try to do that, He will judge you. If you do that and live in that, it means that you're not God's child because He is jealous of those who are His own. He has told us concerning sin in our lives, "For if we would judge ourselves, we should not be judged" (1 Cor. 11:31). And we are also told, "If we confess our sins, he is faithful and just to forgive us our sins, and to cleanse us from all unrighteousness" (1 John 1:9). Sin has to be confessed. You cannot have fellowship with Him and have sin in your life, Christian friend.

> Thus saith the LORD; I am returned unto Zion, and will
> dwell in the midst of Jerusalem: and Jerusalem shall be
> called a city of truth; and the mountain of the LORD of
> hosts the holy mountain [Zech. 8:3].

This prophecy was not fulfilled then, which was obvious to those people. Rather, this looks to the future. It has not been fulfilled since then, and it's not being fulfilled today. God makes it clear that He will return to Zion, and He makes it clear that He is going to dwell in the midst of Jerusalem.

"And Jerusalem shall be called a city of truth." Today it is a city where there are more religions than you can imagine! Every Christian organization has built something there, and there are all kinds of cults and "isms" there. It is not the city of truth today.

"And the mountain of the LORD of hosts the holy mountain." I have never seen anything there that I thought you could call holy. It's just not holy today, my friend. It will be holy when He gets back there, but He is not back there yet. This prophecy looks to the future.

"Thus saith the LORD; I am returned unto Zion, and will dwell in the midst of Jerusalem: and Jerusalem shall be called a city of truth." Earlier, Isaiah had made it very clear that Jerusalem is to become the capital of the earth. In the second chapter of his prophecy, we read, "The word that Isaiah the son of Amoz saw concerning Judah and Jerusalem. And it shall come to pass in the last days, that the mountain of the LORD'S house shall be established in the top of the mountains, and shall be exalted above the hills; and all nations shall flow unto it" (Isa. 2:1-2). Zechariah is here looking on toward the last days and is encouraging the people. They have returned to the land, and God has blessed them to a certain degree, but this is a miniature of what is going to come in the future. There is a glorious day in the future which does not depend upon a ritual or a liturgy or a ceremony or jumping through some little hoop and thinking that that will please God. God says that it is the heart which will have to be changed, and He says that He is going to change these people's hearts. The Word of God will go forth from Jerusalem, and it will be called a city of truth. Isaiah goes on to say in his prophecy, "And many people shall go and say, Come ye, and let us go up to the mountain of the LORD, to the house of the God of Jacob; and he will teach us of his ways, and we will walk in his paths: for out of Zion shall go forth the law, and the word of the LORD from Jerusalem. And he shall judge among the nations, and shall rebuke many people: and they shall beat their swords into plowshares, and their spears into pruninghooks: nation shall not lift up sword against nation, neither shall they learn war any more" (Isa. 2:3-4). But we have not come to that day yet—we had better keep our atom bombs dry and ready for use. You never know in this mean, big, bad world when you will need things like that. Yet there is coming a day when "Jerusalem shall be called a city of truth; and the mountain [or, kingdom] of the LORD of hosts the holy mountain." In other words, Zechariah is speaking of the establishment of the millennial Kingdom which is yet in the future.

> Thus saith the LORD of hosts; There shall yet old men and old women dwell in the streets of Jerusalem, and every man with his staff in his hand for very age [Zech. 8:4].

Jerusalem will be a place where old people can live. People will not have to go to retirement centers or to senior citizens' cities. I want to say something here that I know is not very popular today. These senior citizens' places of retirement are painted to be very delightful places. I have been to several of them, and I may have to move to one before it is all over, but frankly, I do not think they are very healthful. My wife and I stop at a certain one every now and then to eat lunch because they have good food which is reasonably priced. I tell my wife—and she agrees with me—that it makes me feel very, very downcast to go there and see nothing but old gray heads around. It will be nice that in Jerusalem they will not have to have a retirement center. In the Millennium they are going to improve on the method which we have today. It will be a place for old people where they will be safe and welcome and where they will enjoy living.

> And the streets of the city shall be full of boys and girls playing in the streets thereof [Zech. 8:5].

This means they will not have automobiles, and we will get rid of the smog and the pollution. There are not going to be any cars, and the streets of Jerusalem will be playgrounds for the boys and girls. Jerusalem will be a place for old people and for young people, boys and girls. I think it's nice for grandma and grandpa to see the little grandchildren every now and then. They don't want them for too long, though. When the little ones get tired, they become ornery like their grandmother, and that makes it a little difficult for grandfather, and so he likes to send them home after awhile! But it is wonderful when they can mingle. It's good for the little folk to have a grandma and a

grandpa to put their arms around them and tell them how much they
are loved. Children need all the love they can get in this world. This is
a beautiful picture here—a picture of old age and childhood in the
Millennium.

At that future time, Jerusalem will be the capital of the earth, Jesus
will be reigning there, and the church will be out yonder in space,
dwelling in the New Jerusalem. Someone will say, "I thought that the
church would be with Christ." Yes, Scripture assures us that the
church will be with Him; therefore, I think He is going to commute
every day. In the Millennium, there will not be all the tie-up on the
freeways that we have today. I do not think it will take Him more than
a couple of seconds—maybe not even that long—to commute between
the New Jerusalem in space and the city of Jerusalem, the capital of the
earth.

> **Thus saith the LORD of hosts; If it be marvellous in the
> eyes of the remnant of this people in these days, should
> it also be marvellous in mine eyes? saith the LORD of
> hosts [Zech. 8:6].**

When the delegation came down to Jerusalem from Bethel, they were
greatly impressed. The temple was being rebuilt, many of the people
had built their homes, and there was an air of prosperity in Jerusalem.
They said, "My, it does look like God is really moving here." And God
says, "You don't see what I see in the future. You think that this is
something wonderful, but this is nothing compared to what it is going
to be like in the future."

Notice again how often the words, "the LORD of hosts" or "the LORD
of armies," occur—

> **Thus saith the LORD of hosts; Behold, I will save my peo-
> ple from the east country, and from the west country
> [Zech. 8:7].**

This is quite interesting. "The east country" is the place from which
the remnant had returned. A great many come out of Yemen even in

our day, and I am told that there are still great numbers of Jews in the Orient. God says, "I will bring My people from the east country and from the west country." Where is "the west country"? My nation is part of it, I think. When I take a plane from Jerusalem, it flies out toward the west and just keeps going west until I finally get back to Los Angeles. The Jews will be leaving this country someday. Just think what New York City will become. It will practically become a ghost town because there are more Jews there than there are in Israel today. God is going to bring His people back to the land of Israel. He is telling the people of Zechariah's day, "If you of the remnant think that what you see is wonderful, think of what I see out yonder in the future."

And I will bring them, and they shall dwell in the midst of Jerusalem: and they shall be my people, and I will be their God in truth and in righteousness [Zech. 8:8].

The Jews are not His people now. Somebody asks me, "Do you believe that the Jews are God's chosen people?" I probably shock them a little when I say, "No, I don't think so." God's chosen people today are the church. Peter writes, ". . . ye are a chosen generation, a royal priesthood, an holy nation, a peculiar people . . ." (1 Pet. 2:9). What is Peter talking about? The church—that is, he is talking about the body of believers in which both Jew and Gentile have been brought together and made one in Christ. The only real brotherhood that there can be in this world today is in the church of Jesus Christ. Someday the church will be removed from the earth, and then God will take His chosen people, the Jews, and return them to their land.

We have already seen in Zechariah's visions that God will cleanse these people. They need cleansing just as we in the church do. The church is a blood-bought, blood-washed people. Why? Because we are sinners. We are saved sinners right now, but we are still sinners. One of these days, I am going to be a real saint. I am a saint now by name, but my life doesn't always look saintly. But one of these days, I am going to be like Christ, and that will be a glorious day. The people of Israel are going to be transformed also. God says, "They shall be my people." When? In that day when they go back to Jerusalem. They are not in the city of Jerusalem today. I have been through the old city of Jerusalem, and it is filled with Arabs. The Arabs are the ones who are living there even at the present time.

"And I will be their God, in truth and in righteousness." They are not back there in truth today. They still deny the Lord Jesus Christ as their Messiah; they do not accept Him. I am amazed how little reference there is to God in that land today; in fact, there is practically nil. The leaders of Israel say less about God than anybody else. I heard an Arab leader say, "If Allah wills it." He didn't seem to be ashamed of his concept of God, but Israel doesn't mention her God today. They are not boasting of Him at all. However, in the Kingdom Age God "will be their God, in truth and in righteousness." And "righteousness" means that things are going to be made right.

In verses 9–19, we see that God expects the delegation newly come from Babylon to hear the prophets, Haggai and Zechariah, in view of the perspective of the glorious future. Also, these people are to keep the commandments. Just because they didn't come back with the remnant does not mean that they are excused from the commandments. They are to listen to Haggai and Zechariah.

> Thus saith the LORD of hosts; Let your hands be strong, ye that hear in these days these words by the mouth of the prophets, which were in the day that the foundation of the house of the LORD of hosts was laid, that the temple might be built [Zech. 8:9].

"The prophets" are Haggai and Zechariah. They are the ones encouraging the people to build the temple. They are encouraging these newcomers to help with the building of the temple, and they did help, by the way.

> For before these days there was no hire for man, nor any hire for beast; neither was there any peace to him that went out or came in because of the affliction: for I set all men every one against his neighbour [Zech. 8:10].

"For before these days there was no hire for man, nor any hire for beast." In other words, unemployment was a real factor in the economics of the country at that time.

"Neither was there any peace to him that went out or came in because of the affliction: for I set all men every one against his neighbour." In my nation today, we have practically forgotten God. There are very few in public life today who make any reference to Him except to ridicule Him. God is pretty well left out; yet we are wondering why we are having all this trouble with the different groups which we call "minority groups." Not only are there the racial divisions, but also there are social divisions, economic divisions, and geographical divisions. There has never been a time when there has been so much talk like: "Let's get together. Let's stand together as a nation. Let's do this as one people." We get a great deal of that kind of talk from our leaders. They encourage us to do this and to do that in order to accommodate this minority group and that minority group. And yet we get farther and farther apart. Do you know why? Because we have left God out. God told Israel, "You're not having peace, and there are divisions among you." Certainly there are all kinds of divisions among us—it is almost warfare that is taking place. There is turmoil and violence on every hand. Every politician who runs for office thinks that he's got the solution to it. The problem is that he *doesn't* have the solution. And I want to say to you, *I* don't have the solution, but the Word of God says, "There is no peace, saith my God, to the wicked" (Isa. 57:21). The answer is that we need to get God back in the picture today. We need to turn to Him.

> **But now I will not be unto the residue of this people as in the former days, saith the LORD of hosts [Zech. 8:11].**

God says to them, "I don't intend to bless you as you are now or as you were before I sent you into captivity, but I am going to bless you."

> **For the seed shall be prosperous; the vine shall give her fruit, and the ground shall give her increase, and the heavens shall give their dew; and I will cause the rem-**

> nant of this people to possess all these things [Zech.
> 8:12].

God brought prosperity to that nation for a period of time. The great judgment came upon them, of course, when they rejected the Messiah—Titus the Roman destroyed Jerusalem and scattered the people throughout the Roman Empire. They have never returned from that dispersion, according to the Word of God.

> And it shall come to pass, that as ye were a curse among
> the heathen, O house of Judah, and house of Israel; so
> will I save you, and ye shall be a blessing: fear not, but
> let your hands be strong [Zech. 8:13].

At the time that I am writing this, there are still fingers being pointed at Israel. Practically all of Europe has deserted them because of the oil situation, and they are finding out that they are not worth more than a gallon of gasoline. It is a tragic situation. They have become a curse among the nations. Anti-Semitism is growing again throughout the world. God says, "When I save them and bring them back to that land, they are going to be a blessing to the world." I believe that the nation of Israel will be the priests for the gentile nations of the earth. They will stand between God and the gentile nations during the Millennium.

> For thus saith the Lord of hosts; As I thought to punish
> you, when your fathers provoked me to wrath, saith the
> Lord of hosts, and I repented not [Zech. 8:14].

"For thus saith the Lord of hosts." Notice how often this phrase occurs. "As I thought to punish you, when your fathers provoked me to wrath, saith the Lord of hosts, and I repented not." In other words, God says, "I didn't change my mind about that."

In this section we are looking forward to the time when God is going to make Jerusalem the capital of this earth. God says that nothing can detour or detract Him from His purpose. He intends to do this by His marvelous infinite grace. In writing to the Romans Paul says, "For he saith to Moses, I will have mercy on whom I will have mercy, and I will have compassion on whom I will have compassion. So then it is not of him that willeth, nor of him that runneth, but of God that sheweth mercy" (Rom. 9:15–16). Moses went to God and prayed about whether or not God would destroy the children of Israel. God said in effect, "I'm going to hear you, Moses, but I'm not going to hear you because you are Moses. I will show mercy and grace to those whom I will show mercy and grace. Therefore, it is not him that runneth—to him that trots through a ritual or goes to a lot of church services—it is the Lord Jesus Christ who shows mercy." My friend, we can say with the apostle Paul we are what we are by the *grace* of God.

> **So again have I thought in these days to do well unto Jerusalem and to the house of Judah: fear ye not [Zech. 8:15].**

God says to these people, "It is not because you have been through the ritual or because you have omitted the ritual. Whether you do or whether you don't, I am showing *mercy* to you." But this is not the end in itself, this time of blessing is a very small thing. God looks down through the centuries and says, "The day is coming when I intend to deal again with you, and in that day I will do a glorious thing upon the earth." He is looking down to the time of the Millennium.

Now since they are going to represent God in the end times, it does not mean that they can do as they please. The grace and mercy of God extended to us does not mean that we can live any kind of life, although some people think that. Listen to what God says now—

> **These are the things that ye shall do; Speak ye every man the truth to his neighbour; execute the judgment of truth and peace in your gates [Zech. 8:16].**

"These are the things that ye shall do." Have you trusted Christ as your Savior? Then you have been saved by grace and mercy. But wait a minute, He says, "If ye love me, keep my commandments" (John 14:15). If you love Him, you are going to keep His commandments. You do not keep His commandments in order to get saved because you *have been* saved by His grace and mercy. The obedience of your life will never add anything to your salvation.

"Speak ye every man the truth to his neighbour." Ours is the day when lying is acceptable in every walk of life. Business cannot be depended upon today to tell the truth. Advertising is very inaccurate. The news media cannot be depended upon to tell the truth. The government cannot be depended upon to tell the truth, and it does not make any difference what party you are talking about. It would seem that you cannot trust men in any walk of life—not the military nor educators nor scientists. In all of these areas today, we are finding that truth has suddenly gone out of style. It is about time that boys and girls were taught in school certain moral standards, and one of them is that if you don't tell the truth, you're a liar—there is no other way around that.

"Execute the judgment of truth and peace in your gates." "The gates" were where the courts of law convened in that day. Many today have confessed that they have lied even to a grand jury, that they have lied when they were under oath!

"Execute the judgment of truth." What He is talking about here is not the *act* of judging. You and I are going to judge. Whether we judge honestly or dishonestly, whether we judge truthfully or untruthfully, we are going to judge. What He has in mind here is the *motive*. The thing that should motivate judging is truth.

> **And let none of you imagine evil in your hearts against his neighbour; and love no false oath: for all these are things that I hate, saith the Lord [Zech. 8:17].**

"And let none of you imagine evil in your hearts against his neighbour." That means that you're not to covet anything that is your neighbor's.

"And love no false oath: for all these are things that I hate, saith the

LORD." Actually, Zechariah is again referring to the Ten Commandments. The Ten Commandments show us some of the things which God hates. They are not given to save us but to show us the things in our lives that God hates. They are given to show us that we need to turn to Him. We have all these bumper stickers that say that God is love. That is great—God *is* love—but God also hates. You cannot love something without hating something else. If you love the truth, you're going to hate the lie. If you love your child, you'll hate a mad dog that comes into the yard to bite the child. You would kill that mad dog if you love your child. God hates certain things—I'd like to see that put up on billboards today. God hates lying. God hates covetousness. He hates a whole lot of things that the world is doing today.

> **And the word of the LORD of hosts came unto me, saying [Zech. 8:18].**

Zechariah says it again—what repetition we have! God wants you to know that He said these things.

> **Thus saith the LORD of hosts; The fast of the fourth month, and the fast of the fifth, and the fast of the seventh, and the fast of the tenth, shall be to the house of Judah joy and gladness, and cheerful feasts; therefore love the truth and peace [Zech. 8:19].**

God says to them, "I never gave you any fast days. These days that you have set up to fast and to go through a nice little religious ritual, I'm going to turn into feast days, days of rejoicing, days of love and truth and peace." These are the things that are absent in our contemporary culture and society. I wonder if it has ever occurred to anyone that if we would go back and teach the great biblical and moral values that are stated in the Word of God, it might have a tremendous effect upon our society today. Some of us believe that it would.

In effect God is saying, "I don't want you to come before Me with a long face and that pious look that you have. I want you to come before

Me with joy." My friend, a lot of us are not enjoying being Christians as we should. God wants us to have a whole lot of fun. I think that the big fun center for Christians ought to be the local church. Someone says, "Oh, do you mean we ought to have a volleyball court?" No, I mean to come together and study the Word of God—that ought to be fun. And there's something wrong with you, Christian, if studying the Word of God is not fun.

> Thus saith the LORD of hosts; It shall yet come to pass, that there shall come people, and the inhabitants of many cities:

> And the inhabitants of one city shall go to another, saying, Let us go speedily to pray before the LORD, and to seek the LORD of hosts: I will go also [Zech. 8:20–21].

This looks to the fact that Jerusalem will become the capital of the earth—not only the political capital but also the religious capital. It looks forward to that time which we call the Millennium. "It shall yet come to pass"—this is something that is for the future.

> Yea, many people and strong nations shall come to seek the LORD of hosts in Jerusalem, and to pray before the LORD [Zech. 8:22].

"Yea, many people and strong nations shall come to seek the LORD of hosts in Jerusalem." I take it that that does not mean Los Angeles—it means Jerusalem.

"And to pray before the LORD." Very frankly, Jerusalem is not an ideal place to go to pray; it just isn't geared for that today. Actually, you see more religion manifested there and less Christianity than any place that I know of. But it will become the center of God's government during the Millennium.

We referred earlier to the second chapter of Isaiah, and there are many other Scriptures along this line. This illustrates why it is so important to study the Book of Zechariah. A great many teachers in our day have zeroed in on the Book of Daniel. If you go to the average seminary library or to any good library, you will notice that there is volume after volume written on Daniel. Go down the shelves a little farther and see how many books you find that are written on Zechariah—there is a dearth of them. I have a friend who does not believe that there is going to be a Millennium on this earth. He doesn't believe that God will turn to Israel ever again or that He will ever turn again to Jerusalem. He believes that God is through with the people of Israel. He has written a book on Daniel, and he told me, "I have proved my point in Daniel."

I said to him, "Has it ever occurred to you that no prophecy is of any private interpretation? You do not study the Book of Daniel by itself. Why didn't you bring in a little of Zechariah?"

He looked at me rather funny and said, "I didn't need to." So I frankly said to him, "Well, if you hold the theory that God is through with Israel, you can't handle the Book of Zechariah." My friend, Zechariah makes it clear that God is not through with Jerusalem and He's not through with the nation Israel.

> **Thus saith the Lord of hosts; In those days it shall come to pass, that ten men shall take hold out of all languages of the nations, even shall take hold of the skirt of him that is a Jew, saying, We will go with you: for we have heard that God is with you [Zech. 8:23].**

"In those days"—what days? This is that expression that we find again and again in Scripture. "In that day," or "in those days"—this is the Millennium that is coming. The Great Tribulation is actually the beginning of it, and it ushers in the coming of Christ and the thousand-year reign of Christ that is called the Millennium. The Millennium, in turn, ushers in Christ's eternal Kingdom on this earth.

"In those days it shall come to pass, that ten men shall take hold out of all languages of the nations, even shall take hold of the skirt of him that is a Jew, saying, We will go with you: for we have heard that

God is with you." Is God through with the Jew? In the Millennium, the
church will have been removed from the earth. You see, the church
could not be here in a period like this. I believe that the number ten
here rather suggests a whole number, that it represents the fact that all
the gentile nations in that day will find Jerusalem very attractive and
they will go there. Why? Because the Lord Jesus will be there, the
millennial temple will be there, and it will be the place to worship
God.

CHAPTER 9

THEME: First prophetic burden; the coming of Christ

We have come to the end of the historic interlude, and we now enter the third and last major division, which I call "Prophetic Burdens." And I have divided this final section into two divisions: The first "burden" deals with the prophetic aspects which are connected with the first coming of Christ (chs. 9—11). The second "burden" deals with the prophetic aspects which are connected with the second coming of Christ (chs. 12—14).

We will see that this new division goes over the same ground that was covered in the ten visions, but it is approached from a different viewpoint. It begins with the people of Israel as they were in the days of Zechariah when they were a small, discouraged remnant attempting to rebuild the temple. God had raised up Haggai and Zechariah to encourage them to rebuild the temple. Zechariah begins with that local, contemporary scene, then moves on down into the immediate future when they would experience for a time the blessing of God. Then he moves on down through the centuries—God had a plan and purpose—to the coming of the Messiah. We shall see the two comings of the Messiah, coming first as the Savior and coming the second time as the Sovereign. His coming the first time had the Cross in view; His second coming will have the crown in view.

FIRST BURDEN—JUDGMENT UPON GENTILE NATIONS

In the first eight verses we read of the judgment upon the gentile nations which was accomplished by Alexander the Great—an amazing section.

In the days of Zechariah some folk could have become a little too optimistic. They could have said, "Well, this is going to be the Millennium now that we are back in the land and the temple is rebuilt." So

Zechariah is telling them, "No, out in the future there is coming another world ruler." And we will see the contrast between that world ruler and the One whom God will send to the earth for His first coming. The world ruler is Alexander the Great, an arrogant, insolent, highly conceited young man but probably the most brilliant general the world has ever seen. Not only was he a tremendous military leader, but he was a great political leader as well. He had a certain charisma, and multitudes followed him.

> **The burden of the word of the LORD in the land of Hadrach, and Damascus shall be the rest thereof: when the eyes of man, as of all the tribes of Israel, shall be toward the LORD [Zech. 9:1].**

"The burden of the word of the LORD." This word burden means judgment, a judgment of God. Alexander the Great was unwittingly God's instrument of judgment. His forces subjugated "the land of Hadrach," taking the key towns, Damascus and Hamath. Damascus was the capital of Syria and still is today. Also, it continues to cause Israel a great deal of difficulty.

The cities mentioned in verses 1–7 trace the march of Alexander's great army down into the Promised Land. It is history now; but, when it was written, it was prophecy. Its literal fulfillment makes it one of the most remarkable accounts we find in the Word of God. This is so disturbing to the liberal theologian that he attempts to move the time of the writing of Zechariah up to the time of Alexander the Great!

Alexander left Europe and crossed over into Asia Minor (modern Turkey), and he took city after city. He was a cruel and brutal man. However, we must understand that he had an army of only fifty thousand men, which in that day was rather small. Therefore, he could not leave any of his men behind to control the cities that he conquered. He had to either destroy the cities or so weaken them that they could not attack him from the rear. He obliterated many of these cities mentioned here. It is interesting to note that Alexander, brilliant though he was, died of alcoholism at the age of thirty-two, almost the same age as the Lord Jesus when He died. In the Book of Daniel, the Graeco-

Macedonian Empire is represented as the third great world power of
Daniel 2, the panther of Daniel 7, and the rough goat of Daniel 8 (the
goat is the Graeco-Macedonian Empire, and the horn is Alexander the
Great himself).

Here Zechariah presents to us the march of Alexander. I am looking at the works of Flavius Josephus in which are recorded the Jewish
wars, including details of the march of Alexander as he came with his
army into the land of Palestine.

> And Hamath also shall border thereby; Tyrus, and Zi-
> don, though it be very wise [Zech. 9:2].

"Tyrus, and Zidon" were wealthy commercial cities of that day.

> And Tyrus did build herself a strong hold, and heaped
> up silver as the dust, and fine gold as the mire of the
> streets.

> Behold, the Lord will cast her out, and he will smite her
> power in the sea; and she shall be devoured with fire
> [Zech. 9:3–4].

Everyone felt that Tyre was impregnable as it was situated out on its
island fortress. The inhabitants were Phoenicians, a seagoing people
who had developed a great commercial nation and had accumulated a
great deal of wealth. Alexander besieged it for seven months and finally conquered it by scraping the ruins of the old city into the sea to
build a causeway out to the island city. Today we can see all of this,
and I have pictures which I have taken that reveal how that prophecy
was literally fulfilled.

After taking Tyre, Alexander moved down into the Philistine
country.

> Ashkelon shall see it, and fear; Gaza also shall see it,
> and be very sorrowful, and Ekron; for her expectation
> shall be ashamed; and the king shall perish from Gaza,
> and Ashkelon shall not be inhabited [Zech. 9:5].

I have been in this area and have pictures of ruins of the old temple of Dagon. That area has been returned to the nation Israel today. At Ashdod they have built an artificial harbor, and they have built apartment after apartment there. Literally thousands have moved into Ashdod. Farther inland as you go down the coast you will find Ashkelon. It is a thriving city today, but it is not in the same location as the old Ashkelon. The original Ashkelon was right on the seacoast, and the ruins are still there today. It is more or less a park now, a beautiful area, but it is not inhabited. It is not a city anymore. It is interesting to see how God's Word was literally fulfilled. Alexander the Great destroyed these cities and broke the power of the Philistines.

> **And a bastard shall dwell in Ashdod, and I will cut off the pride of the Philistines [Zech. 9:6].**

"A bastard shall dwell in Ashdod." It does not say that Ashdod will not be inhabited; it just says that there won't be a very high class of people living there. And Ashdod is inhabited today.

"I will cut off the pride of the Philistines." Alexander the Great brought the Philistine nation to an end. They never again emerged as a nation.

> **And I will take away his blood out of his mouth, and his abominations from between his teeth: but he that remaineth, even he, shall be for our God, and he shall be as a governor in Judah, and Ekron as a Jebusite [Zech. 9:7].**

"And I will take away his blood out of his mouth, and his abominations from between his teeth" refers to the polluted food and idolatrous sacrifices they engaged in. God would take away the idolatry of Philistia. However, when Christ returns they will be converted to the God of Israel—"he shall be for our God," says Zechariah. Philistia will become part of the people of God and will inherit the blessings of Israel.

This man Alexander the Great destroyed everything that was ahead of him. If he had to wait around a few months to capture a city, like he did at Tyre, he didn't mind doing it because he would not leave any strong fortress behind him anywhere.

Now he is approaching Jerusalem. What will he do to Jerusalem? Well, we have a very strange statement here—

> **And I will encamp about mine house because of the army, because of him that passeth by, and because of him that returneth: and no oppressor shall pass through them any more: for now have I seen with mine eyes [Zech. 9:8].**

"I will encamp about mine house," refers, I believe, to that little temple they were building. God said that He was going to protect it from Alexander the Great. God said it, and Zechariah had the nerve to record it because he could depend upon the accuracy of God's Word and believed that it would be fulfilled.

Well, was it fulfilled? Let me give you the record of the historian Flavius Josephus. According to him, the high priest in Jerusalem had a vision in which he was instructed to go out and meet the conqueror who was coming, and so he waited for the coming of Alexander the Great.

> And when he understood that he was not far from the city, he went out in procession with the priests and the multitude of the citizens. The procession was venerable, and the manner of it different from that of other nations . . . and when the Phoenicians and the Chaldeans that followed him, thought they should have liberty to plunder the city, and torment the high priest to death, which the king's displeasure fairly promised them, the very reverse of it happened; for Alexander, when he saw the multitude at a distance, in white garments, while the priests stood clothed in fine linen, and the high priest in purple and scarlet clothing, with his mitre on his head, having the golden plate whereon the name of God was engraved, he approached by himself, and adored that name, and first saluted the high priest. The Jews also did altogether, with one voice,

salute Alexander, and encompass him about; whereupon the kings of Syria and the rest were surprised at what Alexander had done, and supposed him disordered in his mind. However, Parmenio alone went up to him, and asked him how it came to pass that, when all others adored him, he should adore the high priest of the Jews? To whom he replied, "I did not adore him, but that God who hath honoured him with his high-priesthood; for I saw this very person in a dream, in this very habit, when I was at Dios in Macedonia, who, when I was considering with myself, how I might obtain the dominion of Asia, exhorted me to make no delay, but boldly to pass over the sea thither, for that he would conduct my army, and would give me the dominion over the Persians; whence it is, that having seen no other in that habit, and now seeing this person in it, and remembering that vision, and the exhortation which I had in my dream, I believe that I bring this army under the divine conduct, and shall therewith conquer Darius, and destroy the power of the Persians, and that all things will succeed according to what is in my own mind" (Flavius Josephus, *The Antiquities of the Jews*, Book XI, chap. VIII, p. 350).

Then he entered into the city of Jerusalem and worshiped God in the temple. Another tradition says that not only did the high priest approach him arrayed in his priestly garments, but that he also brought along the Book of Daniel and showed Alexander the prophecy concerning him. This so moved him that he went into the city and offered sacrifices and worshiped in the temple. The fact that he did not destroy Jerusalem makes Zechariah's prophecy very remarkable, and it doesn't contradict the fact that Alexander, though the most brilliant general of the day, was still highly cruel, brutal, and arrogant.

THE COMING KING

The next verse is one of the most remarkable in the Scriptures. Generally we hear a message from it on Palm Sunday because it has to do with the so-called triumphal entry of Christ into Jerusalem.

> Rejoice greatly, O daughter of Zion; shout, O daughter of
> Jerusalem: behold, thy King cometh unto thee: he is just,
> and having salvation; lowly, and riding upon an ass,
> and upon a colt the foal of an ass [Zech. 9:9].

I am going to spend quite a bit of time on this verse because it is a key verse. It is the hinge on which the prophecy turns. I hope you will carefully follow this through with me. May I point out first that *salvation* would be better translated as "victory" or "deliverance." He is the King who is bringing victory or who is coming to deliver.

Although all the Gospel writers record the so-called triumphal entry of the Lord Jesus, only Matthew quotes from Zechariah. The Gospel of John gives almost a running commentary on the prophecy of Zechariah. For example, instead of saying "Rejoice," he says, "Fear," which is actually a good, sound interpretation. Now notice Matthew's record: "And when they drew nigh unto Jerusalem, and were come to Bethphage, unto the mount of Olives, then sent Jesus two disciples, Saying unto them, Go into the village over against you, and straightway ye shall find an ass tied, and a colt with her: loose them, and bring them unto me. And if any many say ought unto you, ye shall say, The Lord hath need of them; and straightway he will send them. All this was done, that it might be fulfilled which was spoken by the prophet, saying, Tell ye the daughter of Sion, Behold, thy King cometh unto thee, meek, and sitting upon an ass, and a colt the foal of an ass" (Matt. 21:1–5).

Notice that Matthew says, "Tell ye the daughter of Sion" instead of "Rejoice greatly, O daughter of Zion" as Zechariah has it. Also note that Matthew leaves out "he is just, and having salvation" (a better translation would be "he is just and having *deliverance* or *victory*"). Matthew quoted only a definite portion of verse 9. Why did he leave out certain things and include others? Well, that which Matthew quoted—and also which John interpreted—has to do with the first coming of Christ. The remainder of the verse has to do with the second coming of Christ.

The Lord Jesus came riding on the little animal of peace and came bringing peace at His first coming. He will come riding upon the white horse, the animal of warfare, at His second coming. But He is going to bring peace. How? By putting down all unrighteousness. You see, the world has had over nineteen hundred years to decide what it is going to do with Jesus Christ, and He is pretty much rejected in our day. So God is going to make it very clear that the Son is coming back to reign. He came the first time to die for our redemption, but the next time He will come to reign.

This was something that I'm sure puzzled Zechariah (it is still puzzling some folk today), but Simon Peter made it clear that not only Zechariah but the other prophets were puzzled. Peter wrote, "Of which salvation the prophets have inquired and searched diligently, who prophesied of the grace that should come unto you: searching what, or what manner of time the Spirit of Christ which was in them did signify, when it testified beforehand the sufferings of Christ, and the glory that should follow" (1 Pet. 1:10–11). When the first and second comings of Christ were tied together in one passage, the prophets "inquired and searched diligently," but they were unable to make the distinction. They just had to write it down as the Spirit gave it to them although they themselves didn't understand it. Simon Peter by the Spirit of God makes the distinction. Christ came one time to suffer, to bring redemption; He will come the next time in glory to reign upon this earth. And Matthew by the Spirit was able to make that separation so that in his quotation of verse 9 he used only that portion of the verse which speaks of the first coming of Christ.

Frankly, I think that the church has misnamed it the *triumphal* entry. I was in San Francisco the night Gen. Douglas MacArthur arrived from Japan a great while after World War II had ended. He was whisked from the airport to the hotel in what they thought would be a private or at least semi-private procession. Well, instead there was a public demonstration that snarled traffic. I was leaving on the train that night to return to Los Angeles. A friend had warned me, "You'd better get down to the train if you intend to catch it, and you ought to leave now." So I took my suitcase down to the train station and checked it. Then I went back into San Francisco to eat dinner. When I came out of the restaurant, I had never seen such a crowd in all my life! No traffic could move. I tried to get back to the railroad station by taxi, but the taxi couldn't move. I finally got out and walked from the civic center to the railroad station. It was the only way I could have gotten there on time. The next day the same thing was repeated when MacArthur arrived in New York. *That* was a triumphal entry.

By comparison, the so-called triumphal entry of Christ into Jerusalem would seem very poor indeed. It was actually a parade of poverty. It was no ticker tape parade but was the coming in of a very poor man with a few very poor followers. If there had been a Roman in Jerusalem that day who had stepped out of a building at that moment, he would have asked someone what was going on. If they had said, "This is the triumphal entry of Jesus," he would have laughed. He would have said, "You think this is a triumphal entry? You should have been in Rome when Caesar came back from Gaul. There was a parade that lasted over three days as he brought back the booty and the captives." To a Roman, this entry of Jesus would have looked mighty poor and beggarly.

Well, Christ did not intend that it be triumphal. When He rode into Jerusalem, it actually marked a crisis in His life, a life that was filled with crises. It marked a change of tactics. Heretofore He had slipped into the city silently. He had entered unobtrusively. He had sought the shadows. There was no publicity. He was always withdrawing from the crowd, not courting attention. It was foretold that He would not cry or strive or cause His voice to be heard in the street (see Isa. 42:2). He entered by the Sheep Gate and would attempt to come in eluding the mob, evading the crowd. Even after He had performed a miracle, He put a hush-hush on it. Now there is an about-face in His approach. It would seem to us that there is an inconsistency here if we did not recognize this as a crisis point. Now He comes out into the open. He enters publicly. He demands attention. He requires a decision. He forces the issue. For one brief moment the nation must consider Him as their King and their Messiah. The Pharisees were accurate when they said, ". . . the world is gone after him" (John 12:19). Jerusalem was stirred when He came in. In spite of His pushing Himself to the front, He was meek. Matthew lifts that out of Zechariah's text which says that He was just and lowly. I disagree with several good Bible commentators who assume that His riding on the little animal, the donkey, denotes His meekness. Far from it. That little donkey was an animal that kings rode upon. You see, the horse was the animal of warfare and is so used in Scripture. The little donkey was the animal that kings rode upon when they were at peace. It was a royal animal. In Judges 10:3-4 we see a judge who had thirty sons, and he got all of them donkeys to ride upon. In this day it would be like buying them each a Jaguar sports car. Riding a donkey did not denote meekness. The thought in Zechariah's prophecy was that in spite of the fact that the coming Messiah would be riding in as the King, He would still be meek and lowly.

In this incident there is another false impression that needs to be corrected. There is the assumption that there was one so-called triumphal entry. Bible teachers in Great Britain and Europe have largely recognized that Christ entered Jerusalem on three consecutive days. He came the first time on the Sabbath Day, which was Saturday. Also He came in on Sunday and again on Monday. He came in the first time on the Sabbath Day as the King. Notice Mark's record: "And Jesus entered into Jerusalem, and into the temple: and when he had looked round about upon all things, and now the eventide was come, he went out unto Bethany with the twelve" (Mark 11:11). He just looked around. The money changers were not there—it was the Sabbath; He just looked around and left. His very action was one of rejection. He came in as King on Palm Saturday, if you please. Then, when He came in on Sunday, the first day of the week, the money changers were in the temple, and He cleansed the temple at that time. "And Jesus went into the temple of God, and cast out all them that sold and bought in the temple, and overthrew the tables of the moneychangers, and the seats of them that sold doves" (Matt. 21:12). This is quite remarkable. It is the only action that He ever performed as Priest when He was here upon this earth. The writer to the Hebrews makes it clear that He was not a priest here on earth: "For if he were on earth, he should not be a priest, seeing that there are priests that offer gifts according to the law" (Heb. 8:4). No priest dared to cleanse the temple, but He did when He came back to the temple on Palm Sunday.

Then He came back in on Monday, and on the way He cursed the fig tree, then—". . . when he was come into the temple, the chief priests and the elders of the people came unto him as he was teaching, and said, By what authority doest thou these things? and who gave thee this authority?" (Matt. 21:23). Notice that on this day He was *teaching;* He was speaking for God. He was God's Prophet. At that time He met every objection; He silenced the enemy. His was the voice of God. He said, ". . . he that hath seen me hath seen the Father . . ." (John 14:9), and certainly it was equally true that he that *heard* Him had heard the Father.

So you see that Christ's entry into Jerusalem was not one but three times. His final appearance before the nation was in His threefold office of Prophet, Priest, and King.

We have seen that His entry was not meant to be a triumphal entry, but was it an entry at all? No, actually He was making an exit not an entrance. He was not arranging to take up residence in Jerusalem and reign as King. He sent His disciples ahead to arrange for a room to eat the Passover, but He didn't send them in to rent an apartment. He was not preparing for His reign; He was preparing for His passion, His suffering, His death, and His passing through the portals of death.

His entrance into Jerusalem was not a one-way ticket but a round-trip ticket, and it was part of the program which led to His death, His resurrection, His ascension, His intercession, His coming at the Rapture, and finally His coming as King. The fact of the matter is that the trail of triumph cannot be confined to a ride on a little donkey from Bethany to Jerusalem. That is only a minor segment of a trip which began in eternity past—when He was the Lamb slain before the foundation of the world—and extends into eternity future. My friend, when you see it in those terms, it becomes meaningful. Without that perspective it is meaningless. The One who came out of eternity is the One who came into Jerusalem—". . . the high and lofty One that inhabiteth eternity, whose name is Holy . . ." (Isa. 57:15). As Moses wrote, ". . . even from everlasting to everlasting, thou art God" (Ps. 90:2). That is, from the vanishing point to the vanishing point, He is God.

The church calls it a triumphal entry, but I think it is a triumphal exit. That crowd who followed Him crying "Hosanna" did not think of Him as the Son of God, the Savior of the world. That same crowd that said "Hosanna" on one day said "Crucify Him" on the next day.

One of the most expressive pictures I have ever seen, painted by an artist whose name I do not know, depicts a little donkey in the foreground chewing on a palm frond while in the background there stand three crosses. That tells the story. It wasn't a triumphal entry; it was a triumphal exit. Six months earlier He had steadfastly set His face to go to Jerusalem to die. He moved by a prearranged program, an avowed arrangement, a definite decision. Nothing was accidental. When He rode into Jerusalem, He had come out of eternity, and He was going into eternity. It was an exit rather than an entry. The Cross and the empty tomb were not His final destination. Neither was the Ascension the end of His story. He could say to the dying thief, ". . . Today shalt thou be with me in paradise" (Luke 23:43).

When He returns He will come as King. As we look into the future, we can sing,

> Crown Him with many crowns,
> The Lamb upon His throne;
> Hark! how the heavenly anthem drowns
> All music but its own!
> Awake, my soul, and sing
> Of Him who died for thee;
> And hail Him as thy matchless King
> Through all eternity.
> —Matthew Bridges

As we leave verse 9, I hope you see the importance of it. It is the hinge of the door on which the interpretation of this section of the book swings.

Now we have seen something of the march of Alexander the Great as he crossed what is now modern Turkey and destroyed those great Greek cities. (It was almost a shame to destroy some of those lovely things, but he did it, of course, because he was moving swiftly to world rulership.) Then he made the turn to go down across the land bridge which is the land of Israel. He destroyed the great cities which were in Assyria in the north, then we saw him as he entered into the Promised Land, first the land of the Philistines, then he came to Jerusalem. Everyone expected him to destroy Jerusalem because the high priest there had refused to pay the tribute money to Alexander which he had been paying to Media-Persia. The high priest felt obligated to keep the treaty with Media-Persia. Naturally this infuriated Alexander, and he was intending to destroy Jerusalem. But he did not destroy it because of the vision he had had of the high priest.

Zechariah presents a contrast here. The triumphal entry of Alexander into Jerusalem was something to behold. Then here comes Jesus riding into Jerusalem on a little donkey. And Jesus is not coming to destroy the world; He is coming to *save* the world. He is not coming to form a great kingdom and attract a great following that would minister to Him. "For even the Son of man came not to be ministered unto, but to minister, and to give his life a ransom for many" (Mark 10:45).

As we have said, when Jesus came into Jerusalem as Israel's King, it was not a triumphal entry; it was an exit. He was getting ready to leave. But He will be coming back. The world will have had a long time to decide what they are going to do with Jesus. They have to make a decision concerning Him.

He is coming someday to bring peace to the world. So He says—

> And I will cut off the chariot from Ephraim, and the horse from Jerusalem, and the battle bow shall be cut off: and he shall speak peace unto the heathen: and his dominion shall be from sea even to sea, and from the river even to the ends of the earth [Zech. 9:10].

"Ephraim" represents the northern kingdom, "Jerusalem" the southern kingdom—one went into Assyrian captivity, the other into Babylonian captivity. However, they are one people and will be reunited under Christ's rule.

"I will cut off the chariot . . . the horse . . . the battle bow." These stand for the whole class of offensive weapons. The Jews won't need their armaments anymore.

"He shall speak peace unto the heathen [nations]." This earth, my friend, will never have peace until Jesus Christ comes and establishes peace. I always shiver when I hear each succeeding president of my nation talk about bringing peace to the world. None of them has been willing to recognize that he is not able to bring peace to the world. Only Jesus Christ can bring world peace—it is just as simple as that. For this reason we have armed soldiers throughout the world today, and we have fought two terrible wars since World War II—in Korea and Vietnam. I agree that we should stay prepared, but we are not going to bring peace to the earth by war. Only Jesus Christ can bring peace to the earth by putting down unrighteousness, and that will not take place until He comes again to this earth. Instead of trying to make peace throughout the world, we just need to keep prepared to protect ourselves because this is a big, bad world that we live in today. We talk "brotherhood" among nations, which is not scriptural at all. The only brotherhood that can be formed today is in the body of Christ among those who have been redeemed by the blood of Christ.

I know it is not popular to talk like this, but I have discovered that the doctor gives me medication and puts me on the operating table and keeps cutting and cutting on me to get rid of the cancer. It is not fun, but the only way in the world that I can have health is by that route. And the only way the world is going to have peace is through Jesus Christ, whether the world likes it or not. There is no alternative.

> **As for thee also, by the blood of thy covenant I have sent forth thy prisoners out of the pit wherein is no water [Zech. 9:11].**

"As for thee" refers to the godly remnant in Israel which was suffering. The best I can do is to make a spiritual interpretation of this verse. The only deliverance for mankind is through the blood of the covenant, and that blood of the covenant is the blood of the New Testament, the blood of Christ. Man talks about his freedom and his liberty. Man in this world today does not recognize that he is actually a prisoner. He is "sold under sin" (Rom. 7:14). He is a slave to sin. In a day in which we hear so much about liberty, I receive hundreds of letters from former drug addicts who have been delivered. How? Only by the blood of Christ, my friend, only by turning to Him for deliverance. He alone can deliver prisoners from "the pit wherein is no water."

> Turn you to the strong hold, ye prisoners of hope: even to
> day do I declare that I will render double unto thee;

> When I have bent Judah for me, filled the bow with
> Ephraim, and raised up thy sons, O Zion, against thy
> sons, O Greece, and made thee as the sword of a mighty
> man [Zech. 9:12–13].

"When I have bent Judah for me." We are looking now toward the Millennium, to the time when Christ will reign. All the nations of the
world are going to bow to Him. My friend, when Christ comes again,
that is going to be a triumphal entry.

> And the LORD shall be seen over them, and his arrow
> shall go forth as the lightning: and the Lord GOD shall
> blow the trumpet, and shall go with whirlwinds of the
> south.

> The LORD of hosts shall defend them; and they shall de-
> vour, and subdue with sling stones; and they shall
> drink, and make a noise as through wine; and they
> shall be filled like bowls, and as the corners of the altar
> [Zech. 9:14–15].

I would say that this is a picture of how it is going to be until Christ
comes. Man is not going to bring the Millennium to this earth!

> And the LORD their God shall save them in that day as
> the flock of his people: for they shall be as the stones of a
> crown, lifted up as an ensign upon his land [Zech.
> 9:16].

"In that day" is an expression which Zechariah will use a great deal
in chapter 12. "That day" is the Day of the Lord, which will begin
after the church makes its exit from the earth by way of the Rapture. It
ushers in the Great Tribulation period, and it ends, we believe, after
the seven years of tribulation when the Lord Jesus Christ will return to

establish His Kingdom here upon this earth. Then upon this earth will be the thousand-year reign of Christ.

"They shall be as the stones of a crown" or like the glittering jewels of a crown. The prophet Malachi tells us that the Lord is going to make up His jewels in that day: "Then they that feared the LORD spake often one to another: and the LORD hearkened, and heard it, and a book of remembrance was written before him for them that feared the LORD, and that thought upon his name" (Mal. 3:16). This refers to the godly of Israel and of the gentile nations. The church, the ". . . pearl of great price . . ." (Matt. 13:46), is not included, by the way. Christ paid a tremendous price for that pearl.

> **For how great is his goodness, and how great is his beauty! corn shall make the young men cheerful, and new wine the maids [Zech. 9:17].**

"How great is his goodness, and how great is his beauty!" This is the goodness of the One who is coming in contrast to Alexander who was not known for his goodness—he was cruel, brutal, and filled with pride. The Lord Jesus was meek and lowly, and He is great in His goodness and in His beauty. There was ". . . no beauty that we should desire him" (Isa. 53:2) when He came the first time. The Cross was a horrible thing. But when He comes again—oh, how beautiful He will be! We speak of beautiful people in our day, but He is the beautiful one, and He puts His beauty on those who are His own.

"Corn shall make the young men cheerful, and new wine the maids." New wine is not intoxicating—it hasn't had a chance to ferment. So what we have here is a reference to abundance of food. There will be no famine or energy shortage during Jesus' reign upon this earth. It will be a joyous time of plenty; that will be one of the characteristics of His Kingdom.

CHAPTER 10

THEME: Judah and Israel to be scattered and regathered

We have seen in chapter 9 the future deliverance of both the northern and southern kingdoms of Israel and how God is going to use them in the future when they will serve, actually, as priests to the gentile nations of the world. There are those who interpret chapter 10 as a continuation of chapter 9. Some very fine Bible expositors feel, however, that only the first verse belongs to chapter 9, and I accept that view.

The remainder of the chapter is separate, which we will see as we go along.

> Ask ye of the LORD rain in the time of the latter rain; so the LORD shall make bright clouds, and give them showers of rain, to every one grass in the field [Zech. 10:1].

This first verse, as we have seen, belongs to chapter 9. It continues the description of the prosperous conditions which will prevail during the millennial reign of Christ on the earth.

The rain mentioned in this verse means exactly what it says—literal rain. You see, God has promised Israel, who are an earthly people, *earthly* blessings. (To the church He has not promised earthly blessings, but spiritual blessings.) The fall and spring rainfall is a very important part of Israel's temporal blessings and would make that land like the Garden of Eden. In our day it looks almost the opposite because judgment has come upon the land as well as upon the people of Israel. The thing that denotes God's judgment is the withholding of rain. I would say that Israel's greatest problem next to the Arab problem is the water problem—how to get more water. Well, the best and the easiest thing for them would be to turn to God and experience the physical blessings which would come through rain. But they have not returned to God, and the rain has not returned.

I have been told that the latter rains have returned to the land. They are getting more rainfall, that is true; but if you are there in late summer, you will see that the groves they have set out need rain and need it badly. There is not nearly enough water to irrigate the amount of land that needs to be irrigated. The latter rains, the spring rains, come during March and April. Although they do get some rain at that time, it is not nearly the amount of rain indicated in the verse before us. During the Millennium God will send them rain so that there will be plenty of grass for the stock and other animals. There will be plenty of rain for the crops and the trees which they would like to set out. The interpretation of this verse pertains to physical rainfall.

However, rain is also a symbol of spiritual refreshment, and it is used that way in other passages of Scripture. For instance, Joel 2:28 has that connotation. That which physical rain does for the land, the spiritual rain, or the pouring out of the Holy Spirit, does for the spiritual lives of these people. Both the prophecy in Joel and the prophecy here in Zechariah have definite reference to the Millennium of the future. There will be a pouring out of the Spirit of God in that day. Therefore, the rain has a twofold meaning.

JUDGMENT FOR ISRAEL'S DECEPTION

Now beginning with verse 2 we have a turning back again to the subject of judgment. Although God intends to strengthen them for the last days and intends to bring them into the Millennium, there are certain things which are radically wrong in their midst. He immediately puts his finger down on what was wrong in Israel. The thing which was really causing the trouble in the nation was idolatry.

> For the idols have spoken vanity, and the diviners have seen a lie, and have told false dreams; they comfort in vain: therefore they went their way as a flock, they were troubled, because there was no shepherd [Zech. 10:2].

"The idols have spoken vanity." The word for "idols" is actually teraphime. They were small household oracular divinities, which are spoken of elsewhere in Scripture. Merrill F. Unger, who is quite a Hebrew scholar, has written several books in the area of demonism in our day and also in the past. I am indebted to him for this bit of information which modern archaeology has uncovered regarding the nature of the teraphim. At the ancient site which is right near Nineveh, called Nuzu, excavations were made between 1925 and 1941. They found tablets which illustrate customs which went as far back as the patriarchs. You will recall that Jacob had trouble with his uncle Laban, and he left with his two wives, Leah and Rachel. He was glad to leave, and Rachel actually took the teraphim from the home of Laban and concealed them. Now, with the Nuzu evidence, we know that the possession of those household gods implied leadership of the family. When she stole those gods, she was getting for her husband the right to her father's property, and the theft was a very serious matter. This explains why Laban was so wrought up over it. He certainly didn't want Jacob to get his estate. He felt that Jacob had gotten more than he should have already.

The second medium of deception was used by the diviners, and the verse before us says that "the diviners have seen a lie" or envisioned a falsehood. Divination is an occult, heathen imitation of biblical prophecy. The Devil has always imitated that which was biblical; he never gets far from the Bible. And every one of the cults and "isms" here in Southern California, including Satan worship, uses the Bible. That is the Devil's method of deception.

It is quite interesting that just this morning there have come in the mail box six different communications from cults and "isms", and each of them has some weird interpretation of the Word of God. You see, every one of them uses the Bible.

The Hebrew word for divination means "to cut or divide." It had to do with the taking of a sacrificial animal, cutting it open, and looking at its liver—the form of the liver and the way that it was shaped. This ancient form of divination was called hepatoscopy. (It sounds like a medical term, and it seems to me that the doctors used a word like that in reference to my gall bladder surgery, but I don't think they were looking at my liver for purposes of divination!) The liver was considered to be the seat of the victim's life, and the shape of the liver supposedly told them the shape of things to come. We have reference to this procedure in Ezekiel 21:21: "For the king of Babylon stood at the parting of the way, at the head of the two ways, to use divination: he made his arrows bright, he consulted with images, he looked in the liver." The Babylonians had diviners (Balaam was a diviner), the Philistines had them, and the false prophets of Israel used their methods. Now God, through Zechariah, is saying that "the diviners have seen a lie." It was demonic inspiration; they were not getting their information from God. God had put down a law forbidding His people to use divination; it was entirely satanic. All the prophets warned against this sort of thing.

Many years ago in downtown Los Angeles, I spoke on the subject of demonology in a Sunday evening series, and we averaged about three thousand people in attendance at each service. Some of my preacher friends kidded me about it. One friend with whom I played golf said, "McGee, you will do anything to get a crowd! Now you are speaking on demonology." Well, I spoke on that subject because I felt it was needed in that day. However, the pendulum of the clock has swung over to the other side, and now there is too much discussion in the church regarding demons and Satan. It is true that there is a manifestation of demonism in our contemporary society, but we need to keep our attention centered upon the Lord Jesus Christ rather than upon Satan.

I am convinced that Satan is out working on the front where the Word of God goes out. And I suspect that the many physical problems that I have had in recent years may be because God has let Satan get through to me. I am sure that Satan would like to stop the teaching of the Word of God today—that would naturally be his priority. No wonder so many of our so-called Bible churches have gone off on an ego trip, playing up some novel program that brings the crowds. My friend, the only thing that God is going to honor permanently is His Word. And during these days I have attempted to keep my eyes centered on the person of Christ. What is the reason for all the froth and even false teaching which is invading our conservative churches today? I think the explanation is that the Devil is out to deceive Christians. And he can destroy the reputation of almost anyone. That is the reason we need the protection of God in this hour as we have never needed His protection before. And we need to keep our eyes upon Jesus Christ. If we stay close to Him, we will be very far away from the Devil and demons.

Instead of centering our attention on the casting out of demons, we need to think instead of *casting in Christ*. That's the important thing. You will remember that the Lord told a parable about a man who had a demon. The demon went out of the man, and the man got all swept and garnished. Although he was rid of the demon, he had nothing to fill up the empty apartment. Well, when this demon got tired of walking around, he remembered this fellow, and he went back into him because he was an easy mark. Also, he brought some of his demon friends with him so that the last state of the man was worse than the first. So, you see, it is not enough to cast out a demon, the life must then be filled with Christ.

You see, when Israel rejected God's messengers and God's message, they failed in their obedience to God. As a result, they turned to all sorts of satanic deception. God says to them through Zechariah, "The idols have spoken vanity, and the diviners have seen a lie, and have told false dreams; they comfort in vain: therefore they went their way as a flock, they were troubled, because there was no shepherd." Israel no longer had a true shepherd to lead them.

My friend, you and I are living in a day when there is a manifestation again of demonic power. A great many folk are judging individuals and judging organizations by the apparent success they are having. It never occurs to them that we are to *test* the spirits. The apostle John warned: "Beloved, believe not every spirit, but try the spirits whether they are of God: because many false prophets are gone out into the world" (1 John 4:1). The need of the hour is not for more youth programs or more new methods in our churches. What we need today are true shepherds who will feed the sheep the Word of God.

Mine anger was kindled against the shepherds, and I punished the goats: for the Lord of hosts hath visited his

flock the house of Judah, and hath made them as his
goodly horse in the battle [Zech. 10:3].

"Mine anger was kindled against the shepherds." These shepherds
were false prophets in Israel who had turned to the occult, had turned
to the supernatural which was satanic.

"And I punished the goats." God is calling the leaders of Israel
"the goats." When I was a young fellow I worked in an abattoir, a place
where they killed cattle, sheep, and pigs for the butcher shop. It was a
very bloody business, and during the first two days I worked there, I
had to go outside occasionally to recover from it. But the thing that
seemed to me more cruel than anything was the use of an old goat
with a bell around his neck. He was called a Judas goat because he
would lead sheep to the slaughter. Instead of the workmen driving the
sheep, they would start this old goat up the ramp, and all the sheep
would follow him. Then the goat would step aside while the sheep
went to the slaughter. Now when the Lord said, "I punish the goats,"
He is talking about the leaders in Israel. They should have been leading their people into the Word of God, to the place where they could
have peace with God, peace in their own hearts. Instead, they were
false prophets, giving them false comfort, and actually leading them
away from God. God said that He was angry with them.

"For the LORD of hosts hath visited his flock the house of Judah,
and hath made them as his goodly horse in the battle." God, you see,
intends to strengthen them against their enemies.

PROPHECY OF THE MESSIAH

Then He looks on to the future when there *will* come the Messiah,
and I believe He is clearly identified in this next verse.

Out of him came forth the corner, out of him the nail,
out of him the battle bow, out of him every oppressor
together [Zech. 10:4].

"Out of him"—out of whom? Out of the One who *is* coming—the
tense is future. It means that from Him shall come forth the corner, the

cornerstone. As you know, a cornerstone is placed in a building structure where two walls meet at a ninety-degree angle. The square cornerstone is fitted in there. This is a marvelous picture of Christ as the cornerstone because, you see, there was the wall of Judah and the wall of the ten tribes. The message is that Christ will be the cornerstone to unite them and permanently bring them back together.

However, the cornerstone has a wider meaning than this. It gives us another very wonderful picture. Notice what the prophet Isaiah has written about it: "Therefore thus saith the Lord God, Behold, I lay in Zion for a foundation a stone, a tried stone, a precious corner stone, a sure foundation; he that believeth shall not make haste" (Isa. 28:16). Peter quotes this in his epistle and makes it clear that the cornerstone is Christ. "Wherefore also it is contained in the scripture, Behold, I lay in Sion a chief corner stone, elect, precious: and he that believeth on him shall not be confounded" (1 Pet. 2:6). Notice that Peter used the word *confounded*, while Isaiah had used the expression "not make haste," meaning "did not get in a hurry, did not get confused." They both are expressing the same thought. My friend, in these days in which we live, what is the answer to the occult, to the satanic? Well, in the first place, we should have nothing to do with it. We are not to meddle with it. Secondly, we should stay close to the Word of God and close to the person of Christ. Here in Zechariah note that immediately after He has warned against the occult, He introduces the cornerstone.

We need not imagine that we are too intelligent to be deceived by the occult. The Greeks in their day were a very intelligent people; yet they made constant trips to Delphi. The way that the priests interpreted the blowing of the leaves in that cave at Delphi would put the Greek army out to sea or would take a man off his throne. It would change the course of history. If you think they were just following a superstition, I think you are wrong. It is my conviction that the Devil was using it to direct the Greek Empire. He was having a heyday. Frankly, it concerns me to hear of our leaders in Washington consulting fortune-tellers and others who deal in the occult. I am afraid that we are getting our guidance from the wrong source.

What should we do? Turn to the person of Christ. He is the cornerstone. He is the foundation on which we can rest. "Unto you therefore which believe he is precious; but unto them which be disobedient, the stone which the builders disallowed, the same is made the head of the corner, and a stone of stumbling, and a rock of offence, even to them which stumble at the word, being disobedient: whereunto also they were appointed" (1 Pet. 2:7–8). It is my observation that the people who go into the cults have heard the Word of God and have heard the gospel, but they have turned their backs on it. When an individual rejects the truth, God sends them ". . . strong delusion, that they should believe a lie" (2 Thess. 2:11). That principle is still in operation today.

The Lord Jesus made a very startling statement when He called Himself a stone: ". . . whosoever shall fall on this stone shall be broken: but on whomsoever it shall fall, it will grind him to powder" (Matt. 21:44). What happens to you is determined by your relationship to the stone. You can fall on it, or it will fall on you. You can accept and receive Jesus Christ. You can come to Him as a sinner and fall upon Him. You can trust Him, rest upon Him. This means that you are broken in that you no longer trust yourself; you trust Him. But if you reject Him, He will become the stone that will fall on you and grind you to powder. In other words, He is going to be your judge.

Daniel mentioned this in chapter 2 of his prophecy. He was given a vision of the times at the end of the gentile world rule when a stone cut out without hands (representing the Lord Jesus Christ) will smite the earth—every government and everyone in rebellion against God. He is *that* kind of a stone.

Now not only does Zechariah call Him the cornerstone, but also "out of him the *nail.*" This is an interesting word. A nail is, of course, a stake or a tent peg used to fasten a tent securely to the ground. In the case of the wilderness tabernacle, the Israelites had tent pins which they used to keep the tabernacle from taking off with the wind. They had to nail it down with pins driven deeply into the desert sand. And here Christ is pictured as the nail or the tent pin. He is the one who holds things down, and we need to allow Him to hold us to the faith. What a picture this is of Him!

Also, that nail or peg was used in another way. A tent pin was used inside a tent to hang things on. Women could hang their jewelry on it and men could hang their valuables on it. This also pictures Christ as the one on whom the Father will hang all His glory—"And the key of the house of David will I lay upon his shoulder; so he shall open, and none shall shut; and he shall shut, and none shall open. And I will fasten him as a nail in a sure place; and he shall be for a glorious throne to his father's house" (Isa. 22:22–23). Although this prophecy was directed to Eliakim, Revelation 3:7 makes it clear that the final fulfillment will be in Christ Himself. He is the one who will become a throne of honor to His Father's house, and only on Him will rest all the glory of His Father's house. To gain Him is to gain that which is more precious than anything in the world.

Notice that Zechariah presents Him as the "battle bow," meaning the warrior and conqueror. He is the one who is going to come to this earth to put down all unrighteousness, and the armies of heaven are going to follow Him. He is going to put down "every oppressor"—the false leaders, both religious and political, whom He has called "goats."

> **And they shall be as mighty men, which tread down their enemies in the mire of the streets in the battle: and they shall fight, because the LORD is with them, and the riders on horses shall be confounded [Zech. 10:5].**

This refers to the very dark period of the Great Tribulation. God is going to undertake for His people and enable them to go through it because at the close of that period Christ will come.

Down through the years when they have rejected Christ, of course there has been no hope for them. When Titus the Roman was outside the gates of Jerusalem in A.D. 70, the walls came down, the city was destroyed, and the people of Israel were scattered throughout the world. It is the current belief of several outstanding expositors that the nation Israel is not now in that land permanently. I'm not sure but what the accurate interpretation of the Word of God is that they will again be put out of the land of Israel and that subsequently *God Himself* will return them to the land. When God brings them back to the land, they won't have any trouble with the Arabs. Their neighbors will not try to exterminate them. Rather, when the Lord regathers them, they will be there permanently and will be a blessing to the world.

> **And I will strengthen the house of Judah, and I will save the house of Joseph, and I will bring them again to place them; for I have mercy upon them: and they shall be as though I had not cast them off: for I am the LORD their God, and will hear them [Zech. 10:6].**

"I will strengthen the house of Judah, and I will save the house of Joseph." The "house of Judah" is, of course, the southern kingdom and "the house of Joseph", the northern kingdom. That is, the whole nation will share in the joyful victory and blessing of the coming Kingdom.

Even in the time of Zechariah, the small remnant that had returned was made up of all the tribes. We know this because a delegation had come down from Bethel, and that was one of the capitals of the northern kingdom.

Now why does God protect them during this interval which we call the intertestamental period? Well, His answer is, "For I have mercy upon them." We can ask ourselves the same question: How did you and I get saved? It was "Not by works of righteousness which we have done, but according to his mercy . . ." (Titus 3:5). God is rich in mercy. He had to have a lot of it to save me—maybe He didn't need that much to save you. But He is rich in mercy; He has an abundance of it. And it is on the basis of His mercy that He preserved them during that period. After the last book of the Old Testament, Malachi, had been written, God went off the air, and He did not broadcast for about four hundred years. During that silent interval the people of Israel probably suffered more than at any other time (except perhaps during the time of Hitler and the Nazi regime in Germany). Although God was silent during that 400-year period between Malachi in the Old Testament and Matthew in the New Testament, we have a very good record of what transpired because of the prophecies given to Daniel and Zechariah, as we are seeing here.

> And they of Ephraim shall be like a mighty man, and their heart shall rejoice as through wine: yea, their children shall see it, and be glad; their heart shall rejoice in the LORD [Zech. 10:7].

Now just in case you think that the ten tribes got lost, "Ephraim" is one of the tribes of Israel. If you want to check on that, turn to Hosea. Notice how tenderly God said, "How shall I give thee up, Ephraim? how shall I deliver thee, Israel? . . ." (Hos. 11:8). Well, God didn't give them up. They are not lost. It is by His grace that they have been preserved as a nation.

"They of Ephraim shall be like a mighty man." The records we have of the intertestamental period give the most thrilling accounts of how the Israelites stood against the Syrian conqueror, Antiochus Epiphanes. His persecution of these people was frightful; yet they were enabled to stand. "They of Ephraim shall be like a mighty man."

"And their heart shall rejoice as through wine." It was a very difficult period, and they were far from God many times, but also there were periods when they rejoiced in the Lord.

> I will hiss for them, and gather them; for I have redeemed them: and they shall increase as they have increased [Zech. 10:8].

It is estimated that there must have been around twelve million people in the land of Israel by the time Jerusalem was destroyed by the Romans under Titus in A.D. 70, which is a far greater Jewish population than is there in our day.

God says, "I will hiss for them." The word hiss doesn't quite express what He is saying. Have you ever been sitting in an auditorium when you hear somewhere behind you a "Pssst!"? You turn around to see who is trying to get your attention. That is what "hiss" means. Merrill Unger gives a translation with a new twist, and it is a good one. He says that it means, "I will whistle for them." I like that. God says, "I'll whistle for them and gather them."

We know that this has not yet been fulfilled because in the very next verse it speaks of their being scattered again among the nations. Although there was a great population in Israel at the time of Christ, the Lord Jesus made it very clear that Jerusalem would be destroyed after He had gone. He was crucified somewhere around A.D. 30, and in A.D. 70 Jerusalem was destroyed, and the Jews were scattered throughout the Roman Empire.

> **And I will sow them among the people: and they shall remember me in far countries; and they shall live with their children, and turn again [Zech. 10:9].**

"And turn again." Turn to what? To the land? No, to God. The Jews who have returned to the land in our day have not returned to God. I am in agreement with the Bible expositors who believe that the Jews will be put out of the land of Israel again and will be scattered among the nations. We do know that there is some disillusionment in the land and that many of the Jews want to leave and go back to the countries they came from. I believe the day will come when the Jews will again leave Israel.

> **I will bring them again also out of the land of Egypt, and gather them out of Assyria; and I will bring them into the land of Gilead and Lebanon; and place shall not be found for them [Zech. 10:10].**

"I will bring them again also out of the land of Egypt." There are very few Jews in the land of Egypt in our day. I believe this refers to future dispersion.

"I will bring them into the land of Gilead and Lebanon." If you read the Book of Joshua very carefully and notice where the borders were placed, you will see that Lebanon was part of the Promised Land. Some expositors believe that when the Bible speaks of the land of milk and honey, it has reference to the southern part of the Lebanese coast, which even today is a very rich and fertile area. Well, I don't agree with that because we know that at the time the spies searched out the land, the rainfall was adequate, the hills were wooded, and there was fruit in abundance. Actually, a few years of withholding rainfall can make a desert. But Lebanon was part of the Promised Land. God certainly has not given Lebanon to the Jews in our day, but someday it will be theirs. If you are Lebanese, you won't like that, but don't worry, because it will not happen until the Millennium—and everything will be so wonderful at that time that you won't mind at all.

> **And he shall pass through the sea with affliction, and shall smite the waves in the sea, and all the deeps of the river shall dry up: and the pride of Assyria shall be brought down, and the sceptre of Egypt shall depart away.**
>
> **And I will strengthen them in the LORD; and they shall walk up and down in his name, saith the LORD [Zech. 10:11-12].**

Notice that the language reflects God's miraculous deliverance of Israel from Egypt the first time He returned them to the Promised Land. But when He regathers them in the future, it will be by even greater miracles—so much so that Jeremiah wrote: "Therefore, behold, the days come, saith the LORD, that they shall no more say, The LORD liveth, which brought up the children of Israel out of the land of Egypt; but, The LORD liveth, which brought up and which led the seed of the house of Israel out of the north country, and from all countries whither I had driven them; and they shall dwell in their own land" (Jer. 23:7-8). In other words, when God regathers them in the future, it will be by a so much greater miracle that they will forget the miraculous deliverance from Egypt.

My friend, I do not think that the wildest interpretation of prophecy in our day would dare say that the present return of Israel to Palestine is a fulfillment of this Scripture. It could not possibly be. It clearly refers to a future regathering.

CHAPTER 11

THEME: Jesus rejected as King at His first coming; the Good Shepherd—Christ; the foolish shepherd—Antichrist

This chapter concludes the division of "burdens" which hinge on the first coming of Christ. It brings us to the Roman period. This, as the Maccabean period before it, was a very dark period.

We have seen that Zechariah is the prophet of hope—many expositors call attention to this. And his name actually means "the Lord remembers." It is quite interesting that his is one of the last voices to speak for God in the Old Testament. And then the New Testament opens with an angel appearing to another man by the name of Zechariah, the husband of Elisabeth who gave birth to John the Baptist, the forerunner of Christ. Again, God remembers His people.

Not only is Zechariah the prophet of hope, he is also the prophet of truth. Being a prophet of hope is not enough, because it could be a false hope such as the false prophets were giving the people. Temporarily, there is to be great blessing materially and otherwise, but out of the west are coming other conquerors—first Alexander the Great, then the Roman armies. It will mean great suffering for the people of Israel.

This chapter also presents the Good Shepherd who will give His life for the sheep. Then another shepherd is presented, the foolish shepherd who will come much later. He pictures the Antichrist, the one who will shear the sheep and kill them for food.

JUDGMENT RESULTING FROM MESSIAH'S REJECTION

Open thy doors, O Lebanon, that the fire may devour thy cedars [Zech. 11:1].

This doesn't sound very promising. This reveals that there is to be a scattering of the people of Israel even after the time of Zechariah. This was, I think, performed by the Romans.

The Romans used the same method that Alexander the Great used—they came down from the north. If you go to Lebanon today, you will see above Beirut a river which is known as the Dog River. There, right at the entrance by the sea, on the face of the mountain are inscriptions which have been labeled "The Calling Cards of the Nations of the World." Every great general of every great nation who went through there carved his name in the rock. I have looked at it, and the translation was given to me. The only one I could read for myself was the one in Greek—I finally figured out that one. All the great generals came that route because it is the beginning of what is known as the Great Rift, which moves inland and extends into North Africa. The Sea of Galilee, the Jordan River, and the Dead Sea are all part of the Great Rift. So Zechariah is describing here the advance of the conqueror who is coming into Palestine.

"That the fire may devour thy cedars." The cedars of Lebanon were famous. Much of Solomon's temple was built of the cedars of Lebanon, as was his own palace. The cedar trees have largely disappeared today. There are very few of them left. The nicest one I saw was actually in a park right outside Jerusalem. It was a beautiful tree, well cared for. The one I saw in Beirut was a scrawny sort of tree, but it had grown up very large. The place where they would grow the best is up in the snow country. In fact, Lebanon means "white or snowy," taking its name from the snow-covered mountains of the area. The Great Rift comes down right beside them. That was a tremendous passageway for the great world conquerors of the past—Egypt, Babylon, Media-Persia, Syria, Greece—and here Zechariah is giving, I think, the description of Rome coming down into Palestine.

Howl, fir tree; for the cedar is fallen; because the mighty are spoiled: howl, O ye oaks of Bashan; for the forest of the vintage is come down [Zech. 11:2].

"Howl, O ye oaks of Bashan." Bashan was an area in the northern part of Israel. There were a lot of oaks in that country—I think we call them live oaks.

> **There is a voice of the howling of the shepherds; for their glory is spoiled: a voice of the roaring of young lions; for the pride of Jordan is spoiled [Zech. 11:3].**

"There is a voice of the howling of the shepherds." These are the false shepherds who had been giving the people wrong directions and a false security.

"A voice of the roaring of your lions" probably refers to the young princes.

> **Thus saith the LORD my God; Feed the flock of the slaughter [Zech. 11:4].**

"Feed the flock of the slaughter." This is almost terrifying! The "flock" refers to those of the remnant who had returned to the land of Israel. But for what had they returned? Although there would be a time of blessing, the conqueror was coming, and untold suffering lay ahead.

> **Whose possessors slay them, and hold themselves not guilty: and they that sell them say, Blessed be the LORD; for I am rich: and their own shepherds pity them not [Zech. 11:5].**

How accurate this prophetic picture is of that which did happen to these people when the Romans came down.

> **For I will no more pity the inhabitants of the land, saith the LORD: but, lo, I will deliver the men every one into his neighbour's hand, and into the hand of his king: and they shall smite the land, and out of their hand I will not deliver them [Zech. 11:6].**

God says that He will permit this to take place because they had not only turned from Him, but they also rejected the Messiah when He came.

> **And I will feed the flock of slaughter, even you, O poor of the flock. And I took unto me two staves; the one I called Beauty, and the other I called Bands; and I fed the flock [Zech. 11:7].**

"And I will feed the flock of slaughter, even you, O poor of the flock." Expositors differ in their interpretations of this. Did Zechariah actually become a shepherd during this time? Was this a parable he was giving, or did he act it out? I personally think that this is a parable in action. Several of the prophets used that method—Ezekiel certainly did. You may recall that Ezekiel locked himself in his house, dug himself out, and came up in the street outside. Here in Pasadena where I live, digging up streets is nothing new. I think that every street in this city has been dug up sometime during the past year—they may have missed one or two, but I doubt it. But in Ezekiel's day it was unusual. In fact, it would be unusual today if someone locked himself in his house and dug himself out! Well, Ezekiel did that, and he had a message when he came up out there in the street. Also he had a crowd. It was a good crowd-getter, and I am of the opinion that Zechariah used the same method.

"And I took unto me two staves." One he called *Beauty*, which means "grace or graciousness." That was the shepherd's crook, the one that he used to keep the little sheep in line. If one started to wander into a place of danger, he reached out with that crook and pulled him right back in line. The other stave he called *Bands*. The English word *bands* is probably a good translation because it has to do with the making of a covenant. That speaks of another staff which the shepherd carried. It was a heavy stick, not like the shepherd's crook but a heavy club. He used it to fight off wild animals and even human beings who would try to steal the sheep. So Zechariah speaks of taking two staves: Beauty and Bands, or Grace and Covenants.

"And I fed the flock." I think that Zechariah did this literally.

> Three shepherds also I cut off in one month; and my
> soul loathed them, and their soul also abhorred me
> [Zech. 11:8].

"Three shepherds also I cut off in one month" were probably the false
prophets.

> Then said I, I will not feed you: that that dieth, let it die;
> and that that is to be cut off, let it be cut off; and let the
> rest eat every one the flesh of another [Zech. 11:9].

I believe here he is speaking against the false prophets, and he is
speaking against the kinds of sacrifices the people were bringing to
the Lord. We learn from Malachi that some of the people in that day
were stingy; they were skinflints who didn't even like to give a tenth.
They didn't like to bring their animals to sacrifice to the Lord. So if a
man had an old sick cow, he would tell his boys to rush the animal up
to the temple, to the altar, and get the cow killed for a sacrifice before it
died a natural death. Then they would pretend they had given the
Lord one of their prize cattle. Malachi's prophecy really zeroes in on
the people for doing that which was phony and false. God, of course,
would not accept such an offering. "That that dieth, let it die." That is,
don't slaughter it hurriedly and use it. He is calling them back to hon-
esty and to be clear-cut in their dealings.

> And I took my staff, even Beauty, and cut it asunder, that
> I might break my covenant which I had made with all
> the people [Zech. 11:10].

"I took my staff, even Beauty, and cut it asunder." Remember that
Beauty means "graciousness," and Zechariah is saying that he is
chopping that staff to pieces, signifying that God's grace would be
withdrawn. You see, when God put His people in the Promised Land,
He promised to bless them and protect them from their enemies. God
was dealing with the returned remnant in *grace*. Back in 10:6 God had
said, "I will strengthen the house of Judah, and I will save the house of

Joseph, and I will bring them again to place them; for I have mercy upon them. . . ." God was going to do this for them—not because they were worthy or because they were obedient. They were disobedient, but God was dealing with them in mercy. However, there would come a time when His mercy would be exhausted, and then He would withdraw His covenant. He would no longer deal with them in mercy; He would no longer be gracious to them.

"That I might break my covenant which I had made with all the people." What does God mean when He says that He will break His covenant? Hasn't He repeatedly told us that He will never break His covenant? Well, we need to understand the difference between a conditional and an unconditional covenant. God never breaks an unconditional covenant. But a conditional covenant depends upon a response from the human side. The covenant of the verse before us is conditional. God's promised protection of Israel against their enemies depended upon Israel's obedience to Him. When they disobeyed Him, He followed through by removing His protection. It is in this sense that He broke His covenant.

We have examples of this in the New Testament. For instance, God's promise, "If ye shall ask any thing in my name, I will do it" (John 14:14) is a conditional promise. Dr. Harry Ironside was sitting on a platform with a young pastor during a meeting one night. A young lady entered the meeting, and the pastor told him that she formerly had been an active leader among his members, then began to run with the world, and that this was the first time he had seen her in church in months. Dr. Ironside preached on this passage of Scripture that night. She was greatly incensed and came to see him after the meeting. "How dare you tell these people that if you ask anything in the name of Jesus, He will do it?" she asked him. Dr. Ironside answered, "Why don't you sit down and tell me about it." She told him that her father had been desperately ill some months before, and while the doctor was up in his room, she had knelt in the living room, claimed that promise, and prayed in Jesus' name for his recovery. When the doctor came down from the room, he told her that her father was dead. "Now," she said, "don't tell me that God keeps His promises!" Dr. Ironside said, "Did you read the next verse, 'If ye love me, keep my commandments'?" Then Dr. Ironside asked her what would happen if she found a check made out to someone else and tried to cash it by signing that name. She said "I would be a forger." So he referred her to this verse, "If ye love me, keep my commandments." Then he asked her, "Have you been doing that?" Instead of replying she turned red. Then he explained that what she was trying to do was the same thing as trying to cash a check made out to somebody else. We all need to recognize, friend, that obedience to Him is the evidence of our love for Him, and this promise is given to those who love Him.

> **And it was broken in that day: and so the poor of the flock that waited upon me knew that it was the word of the LORD [Zech. 11:11].**

"So the poor of the flock that waited upon me" refers to those of the remnant who actually obeyed God and believed the Word of God.

My friend, the fundamental, primary thing for us as believers is to *believe* the Word of God. If you don't believe that the Bible is the Word of God, you are not ready for any growth in the Christian life. Belief in the Word of God has to be settled. And God will establish you in that belief as you study His Word. You may start out a little skeptical and find certain things in the Bible difficult to believe. That is the way I started, but I have now reached the place where I don't just believe the Bible is the Word of God; I *know* it is the Word of God. This is the reason I don't waste my time preaching apologetic sermons. I recognize that most such sermons are needed, and I thank the Lord for young preachers because they generally get into the apologetic field. I spent the first two or three years of my ministry proving that the Bible was true. Now I consider it a waste of time. I like the illustration used by the late Dr. Bob Shuler, who was the great Methodist preacher in downtown Los Angeles years ago. One day he said to me, "If you had a lion in a cage in your backyard, you wouldn't employ a guard to stay at the door of the cage to protect the lion from pussycats in the neighborhood. All you would need to do would be to open the door of the cage, and the lion would take care of himself." That is a great illustration, and I have attempted to follow it in my ministry. I just attempt to open the door of the Word of God and let it prove itself. It can take care of itself. I don't have to try to protect it from the pussycats in the neighborhood. I just give out the Word of God as it is.

Zechariah is saying that "the poor of the flock," the remnant of the remnant, believed it was the Word of the Lord.

THE GOOD SHEPHERD—CHRIST

There would be coming in their line one who would be their Messiah, and the majority of the nation would reject Him. Only a very small remnant would receive Him at that time. For their rejection, the nation would be judged and scattered throughout the world. Now notice this next verse—

> And I said unto them, If ye think good, give me my price; and if not, forbear. So they weighed for my price thirty pieces of silver [Zech. 11:12].

This is a very remarkable prophecy that has been literally fulfilled in a most remarkable way. Notice Matthew's record: "Then one of the twelve, called Judas Iscariot, went unto the chief priests, and said unto them, What will ye give me, and I will deliver him unto you? And they covenanted with him for thirty pieces of silver" (Matt. 26:14-15). This is exactly the price that Zechariah mentions. It is quite interesting that the chief priests didn't want to pay very much. I wonder if Judas had a little difficulty agreeing on the price—"So they weighed for my price thirty pieces of silver."

Over in Matthew 27:9-10, we find something else that is quite interesting: "Then was fulfilled that which was spoken by Jeremy the prophet, saying, And they took the thirty pieces of silver, the price of him that was valued, whom they of the children of Israel did value; and gave them for the potter's field, as the Lord appointed me." You will find this prophecy alluded to in Jeremiah 18:1-4 and evidently quoted from Zechariah 11:12–13. It is credited to Jeremiah simply because in Jesus' day Jeremiah was the first of the books of the prophets, and that section was identified by the name of the first book.

> And the LORD said unto me, Cast it unto the potter: a goodly price that I was prised at of them. And I took the thirty pieces of silver, and cast them to the potter in the house of the LORD [Zech. 11:13].

"A goodly price" is sometimes translated a "lordly" price. I think an even better word would be a *fancy* price. You have heard the expression, "Well, that's a fancy price for such and such an article."

"That I was prised at of them." Thirty pieces of silver—imagine that! They paid very little for Jesus. They weren't willing to pay a high ransom price of several million dollars to have Him delivered to them. No, they would give only thirty pieces of silver. How *cheap* that was.

What did Judas do with the thirty pieces of silver? "And I took the thirty pieces of silver, and cast them to the potter in the house of the LORD." There has been some disagreement on what was meant by this. Some expositors even think that "cast . . . to the potter" should be translated "cast . . . to the treasury." Well, Judas came into the temple and threw the money down there, but the record says, "And the chief priests took the silver pieces, and said, It is not lawful for to put them into the treasury, because it is the price of blood. And they took counsel, and bought with them the potter's field, to bury strangers in" (Matt. 27:6–7). Zechariah had already said, "And I took the thirty pieces of silver, and cast them to the potter in the house of the LORD." That was no accident. This is one of the most remarkable passages of Scripture that we have.

What is the potter's field? The potter's field was property belonging to the potter. When he had clay on his wheel, attempting to make a pot, a vessel, a vase, but it didn't yield to his fingers or it wouldn't bend where he wanted or a piece came off, he would take it off the wheel and throw it into the field. The clay wasn't the right texture to be molded. It was discarded as useless.

In Jeremiah's prophecy, God likens Himself to the potter. God puts the clay, mankind, on the potter's wheel and attempts to fashion it into the vessel He has in mind. But the clay has to yield to Him. The clay that won't yield to Him is thrown out into the potter's field. He can't use it.

It is interesting that the price of Christ was thirty pieces of silver, and the priests took the coins—they were very pious about not using the price of blood for religious purposes—and bought the potter's field as a burial place for the poor.

My friend, the Lord Jesus has been working in the potter's field for a long, long time. He purchased it. But He didn't purchase it for thirty pieces of silver. He paid the full price—far more than any amount of silver or gold—His own precious blood. He paid the price so that He might buy this old world in which you and I live, a world filled with the broken lives of mankind—broken physically, broken mentally, broken morally, broken spiritually. The great Potter, the Lord Jesus, takes the clay that was thrown away, puts it on the wheel of circumstance, and shapes it into a vessel of honor. We are the clay. He is the Potter. And even in these days of His rejection, He is working in the potter's field.

Then I cut asunder mine other staff, even Bands, that I might break the brotherhood between Judah and Israel [Zech. 11:14].

The chopping up of this second staff indicates the complete severance of all relationships between the Shepherd and Israel, His flock. It is as if God is saying, "When you sold Me, when you turned Me over into the hands of the Gentiles to be crucified, I broke My covenant. Titus the Roman will soon be here, and you will be scattered throughout the world." Their Messiah came, the nation rejected Him, and the Jewish people are still scattered throughout the world.

THE FOOLISH SHEPHERD—ANTICHRIST

And the LORD said unto me, Take unto thee yet the instruments of a foolish shepherd [Zech. 11:15].

This, I think, is another parable that Zechariah is to act out. He is to take again the instruments of a shepherd.

> **For, lo, I will raise up a shepherd in the land, which shall not visit those that be cut off, neither shall seek the young one, nor heal that that is broken, nor feed that that standeth still: but he shall eat the flesh of the fat, and tear their claws in pieces [Zech. 11:16].**

Zechariah has presented the Good Shepherd, sold for thirty pieces of silver, delivered to His enemies, then crucified on a Roman cross. But that cross became a brazen altar where the Lamb of God was offered to take away the sin of the world. He was the Good Shepherd who gave His life for the sheep.

Now Zechariah presents the foolish shepherd, who will appear much later in history. There is an interval of time between the coming of Christ and the coming of Antichrist that does not concern Zechariah at all. He is prophesying to the remnant of Israel who had returned to Palestine after the Babylonian captivity. If you think he has in mind the church age, you are entirely wrong. The "foolish shepherd" will be coming *after* God completes His purpose with the church and turns again to Israel as a nation.

Notice how Antichrist will deal with the people of Israel: he "shall not visit those that be cut off, neither shall seek the young one, nor heal that that is broken, nor feed that that standeth still: but he shall eat the flesh of the fat, and tear their claws in pieces." He will shear the sheep and kill them for food. What a contrast to the Good Shepherd who gave His life for the sheep!

The Lord Jesus said, "I am come in my Father's name, and ye receive me not: if another shall come in his own name, him ye will receive" (John 5:43). Frankly, when I began my ministry, I thought we must be very far away from the appearance of the Antichrist because there was not the world climate nor psychological background for the appearance of a man like he will be. However, we have come a long way since I was a young minister. Today, as I look about me, I think

CHAPTER 12

THEME: Second prophetic burden connected with
Christ's second coming

In chapters 12—14 we come to the prophetic aspects connected with the second coming of Christ. This is the second and final division of this last major section of Zechariah's prophecy. The primary reason that this is such an important section is that it is quite obvious that Zechariah is presenting God's program here. In chapter 11, the prophet first showed us that the true Shepherd, the One who gave His life for the sheep, is rejected. In fact, He was sold for thirty pieces of silver—how cheap! Our redemption was not purchased with silver and gold but with the precious blood of Christ, but what a cheap price He was sold for in that day. The Lord Jesus said when He was on earth, "I am come in my Father's name, and ye receive me not: if another shall come in his own name, him ye will receive" (John 5:43). That one who is coming some day is the one Zechariah calls the idol or worthless shepherd. That shepherd is identified as being the Antichrist. After the church is removed from the earth, after the interval in which the true Shepherd is presented to the world as the One who gave His life for the sheep, we come to the time when the worthless shepherd will present himself. He will be accepted, and he will bring in the Great Tribulation, not the Millennium. As a result, we see here that Jerusalem—which will become the capital of the earth where Jesus will reign some day in the Millennium—is under attack by Antichrist, and we see how it will be delivered.

The second reason that this section of Scripture is so important is that this area of prophecy is rejected today by many Bible expositors, even by so-called conservative expositors. They will not face up to the fact that God presents here a panoramic program of His purposes with this world and with Israel in the future. That is a sad thing to say, but it is true. We also have some men who are called fundamentalists but who border on the sensational and lift out certain statements from this section. I don't think that it is honest to lift certain things out of a passage and try to fit them into the events of today when they have to do with the future. Any interpretation must fit into the entire program that Zechariah is presenting.

Chapter 12 deals with the final siege of Jerusalem and the lifting of that siege. "Jerusalem" is mentioned ten times in this chapter, and "in that day" is mentioned seven times. These two expressions occur again and again. "In that day" is a reference to the Day of the Lord which begins with the Great Tribulation period and eventuates and goes into the millennial Kingdom which the Lord Jesus will usher in when He comes again. The Antichrist brings in the Great Tribulation; the Lord Jesus brings in the Millennium. I want us to note these expressions—"in that day" and "Jerusalem"—for they are the subject of this chapter.

There is so much confusion today as to the meaning of the Day of the Lord. Even as far back as 1951 when I was participating in several summer conferences, I heard two other Bible teachers present a very hazy, indefinite, and uncertain view of the Day of the Lord. It occurred to me that if the man in the pulpit is so fuzzy and foggy on this subject, what about those in the pew? Is there a clear-cut understanding of what the Day of the Lord is? What do you think of when you hear the expression, the Day of the Lord? Do you have a definite conception of what it means? Or is it just a nebulous and incoherent expression that is like some sort of umbrella that you can put down over a great many things and it can mean almost anything to you? We hear people use the word glory. What does it mean? When people say amen to something, what do they mean by that?

I am reminded of the Englishman who went into a restaurant here in the United States after he had been here for just a short time. He asked the waitress, "What kind of soup do you have?" She started out by saying, "Well, we have bean. . . ." He stopped her immediately and said, "I don't care where you have been. I want to know what kind of soup you have." Then there was the preacher in the South years ago who said in the church business meeting, "Now we're going to call on the president to share his report and let us know the status quo of the church." One of the deacons got up and said, "Mr. Preacher, I think you ought to explain to us what the status quo is." The preacher replied. "Well, it's Latin for the mess we're in." My friend, these expressions can mean different things to different people.

The Day of the Lord is an important expression. It occurs eighteen times in the Book of Zechariah alone. We find it in both the Major and the Minor Prophets. The Day of the Lord is actually the theme of Joel's book. Malachi speaks of ". . . the coming of the great and dreadful Day of the LORD" (Mal. 4:5). In one sense it is a theme of the Old Testament and one of the most important themes. It would be helpful for us to break down this expression and take a closer look at it.

"The Day of the Lord." Let's understand clearly that this does not refer to the Lord's Day. The Day of the Lord and the Lord's Day are two different things. Like a chestnut horse and a horse chestnut or like antifat and fat Auntie—they are simply two different things.

The Day of the Lord is not a 24-hour day. Peter says, "But, beloved, be not ignorant of this one thing, that one day is with the Lord as a thousand years, and a thousand years as one day" (2 Pet. 3:8). The events that the prophets include in the Day of the Lord preclude the possibility of their happening in a 24-hour day. In fact the tremendous things which are going to take place during the Great Tribulation have made some men actually reject it and ridicule that viewpoint. They argue that you just cannot have that many crisis events take place in that brief seven year period. But things are different since we have gotten into the twentieth century. In one issue of their magazine, U.S. News and World Report took the ten year period from 1960–70 and listed the many crisis events that took place in that brief period of time. There has been a tremendous speeding up of crises in the world today. I do not think that God will have any trouble fulfilling all the prophecies concerning the Great Tribulation period. The Day of the Lord, therefore, is a period of time. It includes the Great Tribulation period. The Day of the Lord, therefore, is a period of time. It includes the Great Tribulation period and the millennial Kingdom, which means that it is over a thousand years in length.

Has the Day of the Lord come? Are we living in it? The Old Testament closes with that day still in the future. The Old Testament pointed ahead to it, and the New Testament still anticipated it. The apostle Paul made it very clear that it was still in the future as far as he was concerned: "For yourselves know perfectly that the day of the Lord so cometh as a thief in the night" (1 Thess. 5:2). The Day of the Lord had not come up to Paul's time, and nothing has happened since then that would indicate that it has come.

Concerning the character of the Day of the Lord, it is a good day and it is a bad day. Good news and bad news can come in one message. It is like the pilot on the Italian airplane who came on the air and introduced himself. Then he said, "We welcome you aboard this flight. I have some good news for you, and I have some bad news for you. First of all, I'll give you the bad news. We've lost contact with the ground. Our entire radar system has gone out, and we have no radio contact. In fact, we don't know where we are. That's the bad news. Now for the good news: We're making good time."

May I say to you, the Day of the Lord is good news and bad news. The bad news first: the Great Tribulation. The good news next: the millennial Kingdom. Both features will be emphasized beginning here in chapter 12. Zechariah will give you the bad news in verses 2 and 3: "Behold, I will make Jerusalem a cup of trembling unto all the people round about, when they shall be in the siege both against Judah and against Jerusalem. And in that day will I make Jerusalem a burdensome stone for all people: all that burden themselves with it shall be cut in pieces, though all the people of the earth be gathered together against it." That's the bad news. But there is also some good news coming in chapter 14, beginning at verse 8: "And it shall be in that day, that living waters shall go out from Jerusalem." There is bad news and good news, and in chapter 12 we will be dealing with the bad news.

We have, therefore, presented to us the Great Tribulation and Jerusalem under siege. This is the time that Jeremiah called "the time of Jacob's trouble." In Jeremiah 30:5–7 we read: "For thus saith the LORD; We have heard a voice of trembling, of fear, and not of peace. Ask ye now, and see whether a man doth travail with child? wherefore do I see every man with his hands on his loins, as a woman in travail, and all faces are turned into paleness? Alas! for that day is great, so that none is like it: it is even the time of Jacob's trouble; but he shall be saved out of it."

Daniel also wrote concerning this time: "And at that time shall Michael stand up, the great prince which standeth for the children of thy people: and there shall be a time of trouble, such as never was since there was a nation even to that same time: and at that time thy people shall be delivered, every one that shall be found written in the book" (Dan. 12:1).

The Lord Jesus spoke of this time, He identified it, and He Himself labeled it the "great tribulation": "For then shall be great tribulation, such as was not since the beginning of the world to this time, no, nor ever shall be. And except those days should be shortened, there should no flesh be saved: but for the elect's sake those days shall be shortened" (Matt. 24:21–22).

THE GREAT TRIBULATION

We have in chapter 12 a description of this Great Tribulation period, and it is presented to us like this—

> The burden of the word of the LORD for Israel, saith the LORD, which stretcheth forth the heavens, and layeth the foundation of the earth, and formeth the spirit of the man within him [Zech. 12:1].

"The burden of the word of the LORD for Israel." The word burden here means "a prophecy, a judgment." A judgment is coming to them—it is a burden in that sense. This prophecy had to do with the siege of Jerusalem which precedes the Battle of Armageddon.

"The burden of the word of the LORD for Israel, saith the LORD." In this section of Scripture which is rejected by so many men today, there is a particular emphasis upon the statement of Zechariah again and again that he is not giving you *his* idea but "thus saith the LORD." This prophecy comes directly from God. If you reject this, you are not just a higher critic with a little superficial knowledge who is able to make very intellectual statements about what you do and don't believe—but, my friend, you are making Zechariah a liar. Zechariah says here that this is the Word of the Lord. He is either accurate and means what he says or he is a liar—there is no "in-between." When you reject this—no matter who you are—you're making this man a liar. Well, I don't think he is a liar, but I think you are a liar if you reject him.

There are three great statements in this verse which give to us a sublime description of God as the Creator of this universe and of everything that is in it. This is a tremendous and overwhelming statement that we have here:

1. He is the One "which stretcheth forth the heavens." The psalmist says, "The heavens declare the glory of God; and the firmament sheweth his handywork" (Ps. 19:1). All of that above us declares His glory, and it shows His handiwork. And it is being stretched out. Quite a few years ago now, Sir James Jeans, an English astronomer, advanced a theory which has been pretty well accepted today among astronomers. I understand that Jeans was a Christian. His proposal suggests that this universe has grown—even since you have started reading this chapter—and is now several million miles bigger. That is really stretching things! You and I are living in a universe in which these tremendous creations of God are moving away from each other, streaking across the universe. He "stretcheth forth the heavens." How great God is!

2. "And layeth the foundation of the earth." God has given particular attention to this little earth that we live on. Man just isn't satisfied that he lives in a universe in which he is the only human being around. So we have been sending missiles out to the other worlds. We aren't electronically bugging them in order to tape anything they might say, but we are sure looking in their front window to see if they might be there. There's been nobody there. God made this earth the habitation for human beings.

3. This is the most remarkable thing: He "formeth the spirit of man within him." Man is a little different creation from anything else that is on this earth. He is above anything that is on this earth, but he is not equal to the created intelligences which we call angels. I think

that the universe today is filled with God's created intelligences. I do not mean that there are men from Mars. (They have now found Mars to be the kind of place that if you lived there, you would want to move right away!) Although we live in a universe that looks as if it's not inhabited, I do not think that God has a "Vacancy" sign hanging out anywhere. I believe that if you moved out of our solar system, you would find that God's created intelligences are in this universe. They are spiritual creatures, and our cameras are not apt to pick up any of them, I can assure you. What a glorious picture this verse gives of God as the Creator!

Men years ago who were called deists—none of them were evolutionists—believed that there was a Creator, and they believed that God created the universe but that He went off and left it. He just forgot about it. He wound it up, started it off, and then He walked away. However, this verse reveals that God did not walk off and leave the universe. It reveals that God is immanent in His universe as well as outside of it. This passage portrays the tremendous activity of God out yonder in the heavens as He moves in our great universe. We live in a universe that is filled with energy. It is man who has depleted the energy on this little world on which we live. I think that God put just enough energy down here to last us until He is ready to move in and take it over again. It looks as if the filling station which we live on down here is running out of gas. This is another reason I believe that we are moving on to the end of this age.

We see here that God is working with a very definite and positive action as far as this universe is concerned. He is that One who has formed the spirit of man. He is our omnipotent (all-powerful), omniscient (all-knowing) God. He is wisdom and knowledge. As Dr. Unger expresses it, this "comprises one of the most magnificent eschatological vistas to be found in the Word of God"; yet it is disbelieved by even a great many who call themselves conservative or evangelical.

Behold, I will make Jerusalem a cup of trembling unto all the people round about, when they shall be in the siege both against Judah and against Jerusalem [Zech. 12:2].

Jerusalem is mentioned twice here in this one verse. As we have already indicated, it is mentioned ten times in this chapter alone. Here we have Jerusalem becoming the very center of the activity which will take place when Antichrist takes over. Jerusalem becomes the center of attack and of judgment.

"Behold, I will make Jerusalem a cup of trembling unto all the people round about." Better words for "cup" are bowl or goblet or mug.

Let's identify when this will take place: "When they shall be in the siege both against Judah and against Jerusalem." When is that? In the last days, in the time that the Lord Jesus called the Great Tribulation period. Therefore, the interpretation of this entire section is for a future day. But it is going to have a message and a tremendous lesson for us.

In Dr. Unger's words, God will make Jerusalem "a goblet of intoxication," "a goblet of staggering" for those who are concerning themselves with it. In other words, they will be staggering because of it.

And in that day will I make Jerusalem a burdensome stone for all people: all that burden themselves with it shall be cut in pieces, though all the people of the earth be gathered together against it [Zech. 12:3].

In effect God says, "You're going to get hurt fooling with Jerusalem." Again, this hasn't anything in the world to do with Rome or Paris or London or Washington, D.C., or Los Angeles or your town. When He says Jerusalem, He means Jerusalem. Although He says it ten times, somehow or another it doesn't get through to us. Some of the commentators don't quite get the message. Jerusalem means Jerusalem, and when He puts Judah with Jerusalem, He is talking about Jerusalem which is in Judah.

"And in that day will I make Jerusalem a burdensome stone for all people." Now that seems strange, doesn't it? Jerusalem is a rather isolated place, an old city, and actually not very attractive today. Despite the fact that it has so many spots which are sacred and meaningful to us, I know a lot of places I like better than I like Jerusalem. I always enjoy staying there because there as so many things to see that are identified with the Bible. But why should this place be so prominent and significant in the last days? How do you explain that? Well, that city even today has become a burdensome stone, but we have not seen the fulfillment of prophecy—it is nonsense to talk like that. This prophecy fits into a program that is yet future, but God just wants you to know that He was not making an exaggerated statement when He said that Jerusalem can become a burdensome stone. I believe that what we have seen is nothing compared with what it will be in that day. It almost broke up the Common Market, it almost wrecked NATO—Jerusalem became a burdensome stone. Consider the list of the nations of the world which have captured that city and have tried to rule it. For example, at the time when General Allenby took Jerusalem and delivered it from the Turks, Great Britain was the number one power, and the sun never set on the British Empire. But, my friend, today the British Empire's sun has set. It went down because they got involved with that city. Frankly, I hope that the United States doesn't get too involved. God says, "Keep your hands off. I am the One running that place."

In that day, saith the Lord, I will smite every horse with astonishment, and his rider with madness: and I will open mine eyes upon the house of Judah, and will smite every horse of the people with blindness [Zech. 12:4].

Again God says, "In that day"—this is going to get monotonous before we finish this book.

The horse represents warfare, and when a horse goes blind and the rider is mad, you are certainly going to have confusion. God says here that when the enemy comes against Israel, He is going to make them ineffective.

And the governors of Judah shall say in their heart, The inhabitants of Jerusalem shall be my strength in the Lord of hosts their God [Zech. 12:5].

In that day Jerusalem will become a refuge for God's people on the earth.

This siege of Jerusalem in which the enemy comes in from every direction is the result of the activity of Antichrist, but God will intervene on their behalf. When they have rejected Him, why in the world does He intervene on their behalf? We will find the answer in this section of Scripture.

> In that day will I make the governors of Judah like an hearth of fire among the wood, and like a torch of fire in a sheaf; and they shall devour all the people round about, on the right hand and on the left: and Jerusalem shall be inhabited again in her own place, even in Jerusalem [Zech. 12:6].

Again I remind you that we are talking about Jerusalem—not about Rome or Washington, D.C., or Geneva, Switzerland. We are talking about Jerusalem, the geographical spot located in Judah. He has already identified both Judah and Jerusalem, and He will do that again here—

> The LORD also shall save the tents of Judah first, that the glory of the house of David and the glory of the inhabitants of Jerusalem do not magnify themselves against Judah [Zech. 12:7].

In other words, Jerusalem would be looking down, as it were, on the rest of the country. People today in one section of our country have a tendency to look down upon people from other sections of the country. I have been very much amused at the reactions which people have to my accent. Many of them very frankly write letters and say, "When I started listening to you, I thought you were just some wild-eyed ignoramous." Well, there are some people who still think that, but the letters go on to say, "But we kept listening and saw beyond that accent." They realized that I had been to school or at least had finished the sixth grade! My point is that this is a tendency we all have. We folk who have been born in Texas have been given the impression that there is nothing beyond the borders of Texas, that the chosen people are in Texas. There are some of my fellow Texans who still believe that, and such is human nature.

Zechariah is saying that if the Lord manifested Himself first to Jerusalem and to the house of David, then they would look down upon the rest of Judah. They would say, "These are country rubes and hillbillies. After all, the Lord didn't manifest Himself to them first." Remember that the Lord Jesus said, "But many that are first shall be last; and the last shall be first" (Matt. 19:30).

We are going to get many shocks when we get to heaven. I think that one of the greatest surprises is that we will find people up there whom we didn't think were going to be there. And there are going to be some missing whom we thought were going to be there. That's the number one shock we will get. Then we are also going to find out who really are the people that God recognizes as those who were His servants and who were doing faithfully that which He wanted done. And they are not going to be the ones we would have chosen. God makes it clear here in Zechariah, "I am going to manifest Myself to Judah first," and that will give Jerusalem and the house of David something to think about.

> In that day shall the LORD defend the inhabitants of Jerusalem; and he that is feeble among them at that day shall be as David; and the house of David shall be as God, as the angel of the LORD before them [Zech. 12:8].

"In that day shall the LORD defend the inhabitants of Jerusalem; and he that is feeble among them at that day shall be as David." David was quite a soldier. If you don't believe that, read the account concerning his son Absalom, or read how he took that nation which was scattered and divided and brought it together and how he dealt with the Philistines. David was a great administrator, a great soldier, a general of great strategy, a man of tremendous ability. In that day, even the weakest man will be like David.

"And the house of David shall be as God." To me this is one of the most thrilling statements in Scripture: David will be like God. I want you to know that there came One in David's line who is God. David is going to be like God. That One is the Lord Jesus Christ who was born to Mary of the household of David. He was born in the city of Bethlehem. Mary went down there to be enrolled because she belonged to the house of David. And Joseph also had to be enrolled for he was of the house of David, but he had nothing to do with the birth of the Lord Jesus. They went down to Bethlehem, and Jesus was born into the family of David. Matthew writes: "The book of the generation of Jesus Christ, the son of David, the son of Abraham" (Matt. 1:1)—that is the way the New Testament opens. That He is the Son of David is the first thing that is mentioned. He is also "the son of Abraham," but David is mentioned first.

> **And it shall come to pass in that day, that I will seek to destroy all the nations that come against Jerusalem [Zech. 12:9].**

There will be a converging of all the nations against Jerusalem, which we see in a great deal of detail in the Book of Revelation. All of these great prophecies are like trains or planes coming into a train station or airport. All of these great themes of prophecy which originate elsewhere in the Bible converge into the Book of Revelation like a great airport or Union Station.

ISRAEL'S DELIVERANCE

There is coming against Jerusalem in that day the enemy from the outside. Why is God going to protect them, and why is God going to deliver them? The reason is given here in verse 10—

> **And I will pour upon the house of David, and upon the inhabitants of Jerusalem, the spirit of grace and of supplications: and they shall look upon me whom they have pierced, and they shall mourn for him, as one mourneth**

for his only son, and shall be in bitterness for him, as one that is in bitterness for his firstborn [Zech. 12:10].

"And I will pour upon the house of David, and upon the inhabitants of Jerusalem, the spirit of grace and of supplications." This is another reason why I do not believe the present return to the land is a fulfillment of any prophecy of Scripture. The Scriptures make it clear, not only here but also in Joel, that God is going to pour out upon them the Spirit of Grace, that is, the Holy Spirit. He will pour out the Holy Spirit upon these people during this period. Because of this effusion of the Holy Spirit that is to come upon them, they will be His witnesses, and He will protect them during the Great Tribulation period. Revelation speaks of the angel who seals these people: "And I heard the number of them which were sealed: and there were sealed an hundred and forty and four thousand of all the tribes of the children of Israel" (Rev. 7:4). This 144,000 means the people that we know as Israel who live in that land. It does not refer to any people who arbitrarily claim it for themselves without any basis at all. This has to rest upon facts, and the Book of Revelation makes it very clear that it is 12,000 out of each of the twelve tribes (see Rev. 7:5–8). If you are going to claim to be one of the 144,000, that means that you are unsaved today and that if the Rapture took place, you would not leave the earth but would go into the Great Tribulation period when they are to be sealed. Therefore, the 144,000 does not mean any group that we have today, but it does mean a certain group among the people of Israel.

There is another large group of people who are to be sealed, but we are not given the number of them. They are Gentiles who are to be sealed during that period. They will go through the Great Tribulation period, and they will stand for God in that time.

When the church is removed from the earth, the Holy Spirit, as I understand Scripture, does not leave the earth, but He will be on a different mission. He then will return to what He was doing before the Day of Pentecost—that is, He will come upon certain people. Zechariah tells us that there is to be a pouring out of the Spirit upon the remnant that will be back in the land. I do not think that, in what has happened over there since they became a nation in 1948, there has been any time that you could say there has been the pouring out of the Spirit of God.

When that pouring out of the Spirit takes place, they are going to recognize Christ as their Savior. "And they shall look upon me whom they have pierced, and they shall mourn for him, as one mourneth for his only son, and shall be in bitterness for him, as one that is in bitterness for his firstborn." This will be the fulfillment of the great Day of Atonement when they are going to look upon Him. Chapter 13 will develop this a great deal for us. It opens with this: "In that day there shall be a fountain opened to the house of David and to the inhabitants of Jerusalem for sin and for uncleanness" (Zech. 13:1). Then verse 6 in chapter 13 reads, "And one shall say unto him, What are these wounds in thine hands? Then he shall answer, Those with which I was wounded in the house of my friends." In that day they are going to look upon Him whom they pierced, and the question will be asked of Him, "What do these wounds mean? We didn't expect our Messiah, our King, to come with these wounds that You have in Your hands and feet and in Your side." He will say to them, "I got these wounds in the house of My friends. I came before, but you didn't accept Me or receive Me, and now I've come back." They will then mourn because of that.

The explanation is given here as to why God is going to defend Jerusalem. He will pour out the Spirit of grace upon them. My friend, that is the only way today that you and I are indwelt by the Spirit of God. You don't have to seek and groan and grunt and think that you become a super-duper saint in order to have the Holy Spirit. All you must do is to come as a sinner to Jesus Christ and accept and receive Him as your Savior. Then you are indwelt by the Holy Spirit of God. Paul called the Corinthian believers babies, he called them carnal, he called them fleshly; yet he could say to them, "What? know ye not that your body is the temple of the Holy Ghost which is in you, which ye have of God, and ye are not your own?" (1 Cor. 6:19). He is the Spirit of grace. He does not indwell me or fill me because I'm super-duper or because I'm a little ahead of somebody else—I'm not, I'm way behind most. It is because of His *grace* that He does these things. And that is the way that He is going to do this for Israel. Since He's been so gracious to me, I'm not going to object to His being gracious to these people.

Israel will know Him when the veil is lifted from their eyes, as Paul put it in 2 Corinthians 3:13-16. That veil doesn't mean that they are not responsible. Any time any one of them will turn his heart to Christ, Paul makes it very clear that the veil will be removed, and he will see Christ as his Savior. My friend, this is true of any sinner today. You are not lost because you haven't heard the gospel; you are not lost because of this, that, or another thing. You're lost today because you have made a definite decision to reject Jesus Christ. This is a false idea today that somehow or another we are not responsible. Although it is by grace, you and I are responsible to respond to the marvelous, infinite, wonderful grace of God. Therefore, God saves us not because of our ability, not even by our faith, but He saves us by the precious blood of Christ. This is a wonderful passage of Scripture.

In that day shall there be a great mourning in Jerusalem, as the mourning of Hadadrimmon in the valley of Megiddon [Zech. 12:11].

"In that day"—aren't you getting just a little bit tired of hearing Zechariah talk about "in that day"? Well, you haven't heard anything yet. All the way through the very last chapter and the last verse, he is going to talk about "in that day." By now we ought to know what "in that day" means. It is that period of time known as the Day of the Lord. The Day of the Lord begins when the church leaves at the Rapture and the Great Tribulation period begins, and then it will continue right on through the millennial Kingdom, to the time when all rebellion is put down and the eternal Kingdom begins. The eternal Kingdom simply continues the thousand year Kingdom, except that it is no longer a time of testing but everything is then fixed for eternity.

"In that day shall there be a great mourning in Jerusalem." This is the real Day of Atonement. The Day of Atonement in the Mosaic sys-

tem was the only day Israel was to weep. It was the day that atonement
was made for their sins. "In that day shall there be a great mourning."
May I just pause and say that there is today a great deal of so-called
gospel preaching that says, "Come to Jesus. He will make you over.
You are going to be a new personality, and you are going to attain your
goal." All kinds of attractions are offered to you. But may I say, what
do you really think about your sins? Have you ever mourned about
them? Has it ever broken your heart that you have been a sinner? This
is the one thing that this poor preacher right now can say to you:
When I look back on my life and see some of the things that I did in the
past, I tell you, it breaks my heart. It is for *that* that my Savior died.
There ought to be that mourning, that repentance in the Christian life.
The one thing that is missing today is that which used to take place at
the Methodist altars in the old days. In those meetings men and
women would come *weeping* down to the altar to accept Christ—but I
see very little of that today. They come down smiling, thinking they're
going to get a new personality. My friend, the truth is that you're an
old, rotten, dirty, filthy sinner in His sight, and even your good things
are bad to Him. He says that our righteousness is as filthy rags in His
sight. And if my *righteousness* is filthy rags, think what my filthy rags
are! If you and I could see ourselves as God sees us, we couldn't stand
ourselves. We would get rid of our conceit and our self-sufficiency.
Oh, how the church needs a real baptism of repentance! This is the
thing that is needed today—repentance on the part of believers, a re-
penting of their sins.

"As the mourning of Hadadrimmon in the valley of Megiddon."
This refers to the Valley at Megiddon and to the time of Josiah. Josiah
was a king greatly loved of the people, and when he died there was
great mourning for him. Jeremiah wept over Josiah as he wept over no
one else.

> **And the land shall mourn, every family apart; the fam-
> ily of the house of David apart, and their wives apart;
> the family of the house of Nathan apart, and their wives
> apart [Zech. 12:12].**

They shall mourn "apart." That is, it will be done in a private manner. Such repentance is something that many of us even today need to do privately.

> **The family of the house of Levi apart, and their wives apart; the family of Shimei apart, and their wives apart;**
>
> **All the families that remain, every family apart, and their wives apart [Zech. 12:13–14].**

This will be a real mourning. What great sin have they committed? They had rejected their Messiah when He came the first time. Think what it will be like when He comes the second time and there are those who have heard the gospel message but have turned it down. May I say to you, that day is coming on this earth when He will come again. Today if you will hear His voice, harden not your heart. Open up your heart and receive Christ as your Savior.

CHAPTER 13

THEME: The cleansing of Israel

You are seeing, I trust, that this Book of Zechariah is a very important book. I have always appreciated it and felt that it is a neglected book. Each time I go through it I learn something new. In fact, this final section is so tremendous that I do not feel competent to interpret it on the high plane that it belongs. I would love to make it mean as much to you as it means to me. Perhaps my feeling is best expressed in the lovable language of the Pennsylvania Dutch: "We grow too soon old and too late smart." That fits my case.

In the previous chapters we have seen a very definite progress through a program which began with the first coming of Christ to the earth. At that time He had entered Jerusalem, and He had been sold for just a few pieces of silver. Only part of the prophecy of Zechariah was fulfilled at His first coming, which indicates that the other part will be fulfilled at His second coming.

He was rejected as the Good Shepherd who gave His life for the sheep. Another is to come in the future. He hasn't come yet and won't appear until the church is removed from the earth. He will be the false shepherd who will lead the nation of Israel, as well as the world, into the Great Tribulation period. The only deliverance at that time will be the second coming of Christ to the earth when He comes to establish His Kingdom. He alone can bring peace to this earth.

It was back in December, 1959, on a Thursday evening, that a Boeing 707 took off from Andrews Air Force Base in Maryland and headed toward the sunrise. That jet plane bore the insignia of the President of the United States. The President was beginning the longest trip that any president had made previously. He was to visit three continents, confer with a dozen rulers, and be seen by thousands of people. The supreme objective of that trip was *peace.* President Eisenhower at that time expressed it by stating that it was an effort to attain peace with justice. Certainly that was a laudable and worthy objective, and he traveled 22,370 miles in 19 days in his attempt to achieve it.

Since that time, every other president has traveled farther in his efforts to bring peace to this earth. But at the time President Eisenhower made the trip, the longing and the prayers of over a billion people were with him because the world *wants* peace. The human heart desires peace above all else. It was very interesting that he went in the season of the year when we celebrate the birth of a Baby, when it was said, "Glory to God in the highest, and on earth peace, good will toward men" (Luke 2:14). Well, I must confess that back there in 1959 I very sincerely prayed for peace. My good wishes and my prayers went with the President for success and a bon voyage. You know, I am sure, that I did not entertain the delusion that the president or any mere man could bring permanent peace to the earth. Actually I got the impression, as I listened to him on television, that he didn't believe he could achieve peace in the world. I do not think he entertained any grandiose ideas. As a military man, he faced reality. But I think he hoped to relieve the tensions so as to postpone the evil day and to make plain the purpose and intents of this nation by clearing up misunderstandings and misrepresentations.

Well, after all the years which have gone by since then, it is still true that the Baby born over nineteen hundred years ago is the only hope for permanent peace. He alone can and will bring peace to this earth. He holds in perpetuity the title ". . . The Prince of Peace" (Isa. 9:6). He has a program and a plan to bring in permanent peace. He will establish the Kingdom of Heaven on earth.

The prophets, especially Zechariah, sketch this program in some detail. In this book, as elsewhere, we find out something of the character of that Kingdom, which we will note as we go along. We have already seen that the Kingdom has a great many physical aspects that appeal to men: the desert will blossom as a rose, the lame will leap, the blind will see, and there are those who like to think of the golden streets in the New Jerusalem. But when we get off on that tangent we forget the spiritual aspects. We have already seen in this little book that the Kingdom will be characterized by *truth*: "Thus saith the LORD; I am returned unto Zion, and will dwell in the midst of Jerusalem: and Jerusalem shall be called a city of truth . . ." (Zech. 8:3). It certainly is not that today, but it will be the city of truth when Christ reigns there. I should add that there is no capital in the world today which is noted for truth.

Not only will Christ's Kingdom be characterized by truth, it will be characterized by *holiness* and *righteousness*, as we will see in verses 1 and 2 of the chapter before us. And in chapter 14 we shall see that even the bells on the horses and the pots and pans in the temple will be holiness to the Lord.

Also, the Kingdom will be characterized by *freedom from fear*— we will find that aspect in chapter 14.

Added to this, the Kingdom will be characterized by *joy*, as we have seen in chapter 10: "And I will strengthen the house of Judah, and I will save the house of Joseph, and I will bring them again to place them; for I have mercy upon them: and they shall be as though I had not cast them off: for I am the LORD their God, and will hear them. And they of Ephraim shall be like a mighty man, and their heart shall rejoice as through wine: yea, their children shall see it, and be glad; their heart shall rejoice in the LORD" (Zech. 10:6–7). It will be a time of great joy, you see.

All of these are spiritual—not physical—aspects of the Kingdom, and the chief one is peace. When Christ comes to reign, He "will speak peace unto the nations."

We have been following in Zechariah's prophecy God's program which will ultimately bring permanent peace to the world. When Christ came the first time, He was rejected and sold and turned over to the Gentiles who crucified Him. Then a period of time lapses which Zechariah does not deal with. It is the church period in which we are living today. When it ends, there will appear the worthless shepherd, the Antichrist. He won't usher in the Kingdom; he will bring in the Great Tribulation period. His world dictatorship can only be ended by the coming of Christ to establish His Kingdom upon the earth. This is what we have before us in chapter 13.

All of this should be taken in a literal way. The reason that many folk in our day think that God has no future purpose with Israel is that they don't believe that God means what He says. You couldn't read the section before us and dismiss it unless you spiritualize it away. If you do that, you do not have a very high view of the inspiration of Scripture. The very center of God's plan, as we saw back in chapter 12, is Jerusalem. In the last three chapters of this book, chapters 12—14, the name *Jerusalem* occurs twenty-one times. My friend, God wouldn't have used it that many times unless He had meant literal Jerusalem. He was not talking about London or Paris or Berlin or Moscow or Peking. He was speaking about the actual city of Jerusalem. It is quite interesting that even President Eisenhower, back in his day, bypassed Jerusalem, and heads of state have been bypassing it ever since. You will find that the better conservative expositors take the position that this section should be interpreted literally. Let me share with you a quotation from Dr. Merrill F. Unger, whom I value very highly as an interpreter of the Book of Zechariah. I feel that his book, *Unger's Bible Commentary: Zechariah*, is the finest I have found. It is scholarly, and you need a little smattering of Hebrew to get through it, but it is a wonderful book. Here on page 221 is his comment:

> Only a literal application of these prophecies to the restoration and conversion of the Jewish nation at the second advent of Christ can satisfy the scope of these prophetic disclosures. Other interpretations ignore the true scope of Zechariah's prophecies as a whole, violate the immediate context, resort to pointless mysticalizing, and end up in a morass of uncertainty and confusion.

I say amen to that. I believe that spiritualizing it is practically a denial of the inspiration of the Word of God.

THE NATIONAL CLEANSING OF ISRAEL

In that day there shall be a fountain opened to the house of David and to the inhabitants of Jerusalem for sin and for uncleanness [Zech. 13:1].

"**In** that day." We have already determined that "that day" refers to the Great Tribulation and moves on into the millennial Kingdom. Christ will come to this earth at the end of the Great Tribulation, and then He will establish His Kingdom.

This verse does not refer to the first coming of Christ. At that time He did not open up a fountain to the house of David and to the inhabitants of Jerusalem "for sin and for uncleanness." Instead, they rejected Him and crucified their Savior. Even Paul writes in Romans 10:3: "For they being ignorant of God's righteousness, and going about to establish their own righteousness, have not submitted themselves unto the righteousness of God."

"A fountain" is God's cleansing power which was opened by Christ's death upon the Cross. At His first coming Israel rejected their Messiah-Savior, and this fountain will be opened to them at His second coming to the earth. The chapter before us continues the presentation of God's program, and we saw in chapter 12 that in "that day" God would pour out His Spirit upon the people of Israel. The prophet Joel spoke of that also. It is at this time that the "fountain" will be opened to them, which will be when they realize the fact that Christ was crucified for them. We have seen that they are going to look upon Him. Remember that this is God's Word, and He puts it very definitely, "They shall look upon me whom they have pierced, and they shall mourn for him." It is going to be a real Day of Atonement for these people when Christ comes the second time. They are going to be greatly moved, and the Spirit of God will remove the veil from their eyes. Paul makes it clear that the veil can be taken away even today if they really want to give up their sin.

You see, the problem with man is heart trouble, not head trouble. No man really has an intellectual problem. He hasn't got enough mentality to deal with the Creator of this universe, with an infinite God. His problem is that he does not want to give up his sin. That is true of the people of Israel, and it is true of the Gentiles. It is true of all of us—let's face up to it.

> And it shall come to pass in that day, saith the LORD of
> hosts, that I will cut off the names of the idols out of the

land, and they shall no more be remembered: and also I
will cause the prophets and the unclean spirit to pass
out of the land [Zech. 13:2].

"And it shall come to pass in that day"—again he dates it as being "in
that day."

"I will cut off the names of the idols out of the land." When they
were in Babylonian captivity, they took the "gold cure," that is, they
gave up idolatry as they had observed it before. The golden calves
were never put back at Dan and Bethel. But they were still using the
little household teraphim and other little fetishes. Even today a great
many so-called civilized folk think that if they wear a certain object or
if they put up a certain little gadget somewhere, it will ward off harm.
That was the kind of idolatry that the people of Israel were engaged in.
Also they dealt with the zodiac.

"And also I will cause the prophets and the unclean spirit to pass
out of the land." The "prophets" are, of course, the false prophets. The
"unclean spirit" refers to demons. We live in a world where demons
are very active, and attention is being called to them at the present
time. It may be that we are seeing an outbreak of demonic activity as
we draw near the end of the age, but, candidly, I think there has been a
subtle manifestation of them all along. The reason this passage is so
important is that it is the only place that speaks of the demons being
put out of this earth during the Millennium. The Book of Revelation
tells about the false prophet and the Antichrist being put out of the
earth: "And the beast was taken, and with him the false prophet that
wrought miracles before him, with which he deceived them that had
received the mark of the beast, and them that worshipped his image.
These both were cast alive into a lake of fire burning with brimstone"
(Rev. 19:20). And Satan will be bound during the millennial period
(see Rev. 20:1–3). So we know that the false prophet and the Antichrist will be in the lake of fire and the Devil will be bound in the
bottomless pit. Nothing is said in the Book of Revelation about the
final casting out of demons, but it is logical to believe that it will be
done at this time also and that they will be put in one place or the
other. At least we know that they will be removed from the earth.

You would think that once a people had been delivered from paganism and heathenism, they would not go back to it. But in our day the world is going back to it because the human family is gradually moving into the darkness again due to a lack of knowledge of the Word of God. And this is the explanation for the demonic dynamic being manifested in our day. Ignorance of God's Word gives energy to the occult—there is no energy shortage in that particular connection.

What a different world this will be when there is a complete extermination of idolatry and demons are removed from the entire earth.

> **And it shall come to pass, that when any shall yet prophesy, then his father and his mother that begat him shall say unto him, Thou shalt not live; for thou speakest lies in the name of the Lord: and his father and his mother that begat him shall thrust him through when he prophesieth [Zech. 13:3].**

That seems like strong language, but the day is coming, my friend, when God's children are going to put Him first. They betrayed Him the first time He came, and He is being betrayed in our day, but in that future day they are going to be faithful to Him even if the one who prophesies falsely is their own son.

> **And it shall come to pass in that day, that the prophets shall be ashamed every one of his vision, when he hath prophesied; neither shall they wear a rough garment to deceive [Zech. 13:4].**

There are two things that interest me here. First, when the Lord comes the false prophets will be ashamed, deeply convicted, of their deceptive "vision." They will be disgraced because the Lord Jesus has come and made liars out of every one of them. The second thing that we note is that "neither shall they wear a rough garment to deceive." The garment worn by prophets was a mantle of rough, untanned sheepskin or goatskin or a cloak of camel's hair. (When Esau was born it is said that he looked like this kind of hairy garment!) The prophet Elijah wore this type of mantle, and it was this mantle that fell upon his successor, Elisha. It was a garment which distinguished a man as a prophet of God, and the false prophets will feel guilty about trying to impersonate a true prophet. You see, Zechariah was not introducing something new but something that was very familiar to the folk of his day.

> But he shall say, I am no prophet, I am an husbandman;
> for man taught me to keep cattle from my youth [Zech.
> 13:5].

The men who were false prophets will go back to the farm.

The next two verses are startling. In fact, the critics have tried to eliminate them from the text because they say that it is shocking to find this prophecy given at this time. And it is! That is the wonder of it. Certainly it is no excuse to reject it; it is there to *alert* us. I should mention that there is a difference of opinion as to who is addressed in this verse. I believe that it is Christ.

> And one shall say unto him, What are these wounds in
> thine hands? Then he shall answer, Those with which I
> was wounded in the house of my friends [Zech. 13:6].

"Wounded in the house of my friends" has been translated by some of the higher critics as "wounded in the house of those who loved me." Well, they didn't *love* Him the first time He came—they hated Him. Scripture says that they hated Him without cause. "He came unto his own, and his own received him not" (John 1:11). But to as many as received Him at that time He gave the authority to become sons of God. Well, when the Spirit is poured out, they (that is, the remnant) are going to receive Him. And they will wonder, saying, "Where did you get those wounds in your hands?" He will answer, "I was wounded here when I came the first time." He came to His own people, the Jewish race (remember that the woman of Samaria recognized Him as a Jew). These were His people, and only a remnant received Him at that time. And, actually, it will be only a remnant who will receive him at His second coming although I think it will be a much larger remnant. "And one shall say unto him" probably refers to the spokesman for the remnant, just as Peter spoke for the other apostles when he said to Jesus, ". . . Thou art the Christ, the Son of the living God" (Matt. 16:16).

There is a song in which Jesus is called "the Stranger of Galilee." I don't know about you, but I don't like that song. He is not the stranger of Galilee to those who know Him. When He came the first time He was the stranger of Galilee to them. Certainly He is not the stranger of Galilee to Christians in this age in which we live, and I don't think we should sing that song. To know Him is life eternal. The apostle Paul at the end of his life wrote, "That I may know him, and the power of his resurrection, and the fellowship of his sufferings, being made conformable unto his death" (Phil. 3:10). But it is true that they did not know Jesus when He came the first time.

This matter of mistaken identity has been the source of plots for writers of both comedy and tragedy down through the years. Shakespeare used it in The Comedy of Errors. Dickens used it in The Tale of Two Cities. Many dramatic productions are based upon this idea—Alexandre Dumas' The Count of Monte Cristo, for example. It becomes even more tragic when it is a real life story. I read of a mother who had not seen her daughter for seventeen years, and when she went to meet her in New York, she walked right past her. It took some time to meet again because the mother didn't recognize her own daughter. In Reedley, California, I met a mother who had come from Russia and had not seen her daughter since she was a baby—of course she wouldn't be able to recognize her.

However, I think that the greatest tragedy of the ages is expressed in just eleven words: "He came unto His own, and His own received him not." What a picture! John the Baptist elaborated upon it when he said, ". . . I baptize with water: but there standeth one among you, whom ye know not" (John 1:26, italics mine). And the Lord Jesus Himself said that they knew not the time of their visitation—what a tremendous statement! And Paul wrote: "But their minds were blinded: for until this day remaineth [notice that!] the same veil untaken away in the reading of the old testament; which veil is done away in Christ. But even unto this day, when Moses is read, the veil is upon their heart" (2 Cor. 3:14–15). Notice that the veil is upon their heart—but when the heart is right, they can turn to Him. He is a stranger only to those who do not know Him as Savior. Zechariah speaks of this. In His first coming they didn't know Him.

There is a striking contrast between the first and second comings of Christ. Redemption is the high word of His first coming; *revelation* is the high word of His second coming. It was *reconciliation* at His first coming and *recognition* at His second coming. It was the *Incarnation* at His first coming and *identification* at His second coming. It was the *mystery* at His first coming, and it will be *manifestation* at His second coming. At His first coming it was *propitiation;* at His second coming it will be *proclamation.* What a picture this gives of Christ!

THE SMITTEN SHEPHERD AND THE
SCATTERED SHEEP

Awake, O sword, against my shepherd, and against the man that is my fellow, saith the LORD of hosts: smite the shepherd, and the sheep shall be scattered: and I will turn mine hand upon the little ones [Zech. 13:7].

This refers to the time that He was smitten. In fact, when Christ was here the first time, He said that this verse applied to Himself, as we shall see. We immediately identify this remarkable passage of Scripture with ". . . they shall look upon me whom they have pierced, and they shall mourn for him . . ." of Zechariah 12:10.

"Awake, O sword, against my shepherd, and against the man that is my fellow, saith the LORD of hosts." The Lord God is the speaker, and Christ, the Messiah, is the person spoken of. The phrase, "the man that is my fellow" would be better translated, "the man my equal" or "the man of my union." This is an unmistakable Old Testament reference to the deity of Christ.

"Smite the shepherd, and the sheep shall be scattered." Who

would have thought that this would refer to the Lord Jesus Christ? We know it does because Jesus Himself quotes it. "Then saith Jesus unto them, All ye shall be offended because of me this night: for it is written, I will smite the shepherd, and the sheep of the flock shall be scattered abroad" (Matt. 26:31). You see that He makes it applicable to Himself. If you doubt that God has a future purpose for Israel, you need to note this carefully. In the prophecies that we have here which relate to the first and second comings of Christ, did the Lord Jesus lie? He says that Zechariah was referring to Him when he said, "Smite the shepherd, and the sheep shall be scattered." And when He comes the second time, they will ask, "What are these wounds, these nail prints, in Your hands?" And His answer will be, "I received these in the house of My friends." And, as we saw in chapter 12, "They shall look upon me whom they have pierced, and they shall mourn for him, as one mourneth for his only son." This will be the great Day of Atonement for the Jewish people, and obviously it is for a future time.

The final two verses of this chapter refer to the Great Tribulation period.

> And it shall come to pass, that in all the land, saith the LORD, two parts therein shall be cut off and die; but the third shall be left therein [Zech. 13:8].

"The third shall be left therein" refers to the same remnant that shall ask, "What are these wounds in thine hands?" They will have come through the horrors of the Great Tribulation period in which two-thirds of their people have perished.

> And I will bring the third part through the fire, and will refine them as silver is refined, and will try them as gold is tried: they shall call on my name, and I will hear them: I will say, It is my people: and they shall say, The LORD is my God [Zech. 13:9].

Isn't that a wonderful statement? These are the ones who will take a stand for Christ and will be faithful to Him. They will make it through the Great Tribulation because He has sealed them (see Rev. 7:1-8). Then we see them again in Revelation 14: "And I looked, and, lo, a Lamb stood on the mount Sion, and with him an hundred forty and four thousand, having his Father's name written in their foreheads. . . . And they sung as it were a new song before the throne, and before the four beasts, and the elders: and no man could learn that song but the hundred and forty and four thousand, which were redeemed from the earth" (Rev. 14:1, 3).

CHAPTER 14

THEME: The second coming of Christ, the Messiah

Chapter 14 concludes the second division of the last section of the Book of Zechariah. This last section, chapters 9—14, deals with prophetic burdens. There was the first burden, dealing with the prophetic aspects connected with the *first* coming of Christ (chs. 9—11). In the second and last division (chs. 12—14), we have the second burden in which we have the prophetic aspects connected with the second coming of Christ. This final chapter just gathers together everything and ties up any loose strings there might be.

The very interesting thing is that we have had a very definite program given to us in the Book of Zechariah, and that has been true in all three of its major divisions. We had the ten visions, then the historic interlude, and now this last major division of prophetic burdens. We always start where Israel was at that particular time (and they were in a certain amount of difficulty), and then we move through the national conversion of Israel when the nation will turn to God and there will be a pouring out of the Spirit of God. All of this prepares the scene for the return of Messiah, because at that time they have entered the Great Tribulation period.

This last chapter is a great climactic chapter, but it also follows the entire program that has been given to us in Zechariah. This is a section that leads up to and into the establishment of the Kingdom at the second coming of Christ. In each of these major divisions, Zechariah, encouraging the people of that day, looks on to the future and outlines a prophetic program.

There are certain things which we need to make clear about this chapter. The first is that it is *wholly prophetic*—it is entirely that. The other is that it has no prophecy which is being fulfilled in this present age. In other words, it is speaking of *the end of the age* that ushers in the Kingdom. You will find that many commentators, especially of the higher critical school (and I believe that largely all amillennialists follow this same plan and purpose), teach that this does not actually speak of prophecy, that it is not literal, and that it can be fitted into the present age. Believe me, that leads to some strange interpretations! Lowe and DeWette, who belonged to that camp, both said: "This chapter defies all historical explanation." We can certainly say amen to that, as nothing like this has ever happened in the past. Therefore, this chapter is entirely prophetic; that is, it is prophetic from where we are today, and it looks to the future.

The only interpretation of this chapter which will satisfy is a literal interpretation; that is the only one that will give the meaning. And any interpretation must be in harmony with the context. In interpreting prophecy or interpreting Scripture anywhere, you cannot disregard the context before and after. Also, you must interpret this in keeping with the spirit and the feel of the entire Word of God. You absolutely cannot reach in here and come out with some wild interpretation that has no basis in fact. I believe that this is a very, very important passage of Scripture, because it demonstrates the difference between literal interpretation of Scripture and that which spiritualizes or mysticalizes it, making it mean practically nothing at all. Such interpretation merely makes this passage something that is allegorical or something that is mythical or something that actually can be dissipated into thin air. It is an attempt to explain it away rather than to explain it.

Let me make a suggestion that is really a mean one. If you are wanting to know the position of a pastor whom you're not sure about, if you really want to know what he *believes*, take the fourteenth chapter of Zechariah to him and ask him to explain it to you. You will find out what a man really believes when he deals with this chapter.

Certain of the liberal commentators, actually great scholars of the past, and Hengstenberg specifically, refer chapter 14 "to the whole of the Messianic era." What he really means is that it refers to this church period today. You cannot, by the wildest kind of interpretation, fit that in. That is the reason he does not go into detail. Leupold, another outstanding liberal scholar, says:

Our verses do not, therefore, apply to any one situation.
They do not describe a siege, capture, and captivity which actually occurred. By means of a figure they describe a situation
which obtains continually through New Testament times.
God's people shall continually be antagonized and suffer bitter
adversity at the hands of their foes and shall in consequence be
brought low; but there shall always be an imperishable remnant, and that not so extremely small.

Would you tell me what he really means by that? He means that he
doesn't know what to do with this chapter at all. So the thing he does
is spiritualize it—he spreads it out like butter on toast, and it melts
just about the same way!

May I say that these verses are not just figurative, they do not apply
to New Testament times, and the remnant that is spoken of here—it's
been made clear to us in this book—is a *Jewish* remnant. We need to
recognize that this chapter is entirely eschatological.

There have been other scholars who identify this chapter with "the
error of so-called 'Jewish Chiliasm.'" The fact of the matter is, as Dr.
Unger goes on to say, " 'Jewish Chiliasm' was wrong *only in the fact
that it overlooked the prophesied rejection and death of the Messiah as
the indispensable prelude to His manifestation in kingdom glory.*"

With that as a background, let us come to the text itself—

**Behold, the day of the LORD cometh, and thy spoil shall
be divided in the midst of thee [Zech. 14:1].**

"Behold, the day of the LORD cometh"—this would make a good headline for the newspaper. Many times, when you get down into an article, it moves behind the headline and gives you the preliminaries that
led up to the headline. That is what happens here.

"Behold, the day of LORD." Here we are again with this very impressive statement. We will find that the thing which is before us in
these first three verses is the last siege of Jerusalem. Then in verses
4–7, we have the personal advent of the Messiah. We have seen all of
this in other chapters of Zechariah, but now we have it brought in

from a little different angle. For instance, regarding the Great Tribulation period and the siege of Jerusalem, the thing that was important in the other passages was an emphasis on the latter part of the Tribulation and the deliverance that came, and Zechariah was prophesying to the people for their encouragement. But here we see how tragic it is actually going to be during that period of the Day of the Lord. The thing that Joel had said was that the Day of the Lord is not light; it is darkness. It begins in darkness. The hopelessness and the helplessness of these people in that period is difficult for us to understand.

"Behold, the day of the LORD cometh." The Hebrew idiom that is employed here is *yomba' leyahweh*. (I pass that on to you just to let you know that I did study Hebrew, although I've forgotten most of it by now.) This is the expression that is headline material here, and it refers to this coming day which is yet in the future (after the church is removed) when Antichrist brings on the Great Tribulation, although the world will believe that he is bringing in the Millennium. We certainly have had quite a few presidents in my day who were going to bring in the Millennium. Not one of them has gotten within four miles of the Millennium, but that does not prevent Americans from believing that the candidate is going to do it. Well, none of them is going to do it—only Jesus Christ can do that.

Dr. Unger's rendering of this verse is: "Lo, a day is coming—the Lord's—when thy spoil shall be distributed in the midst of thee." The enemy is going to take Jerusalem again, and this will be the last siege.

> For I will gather all nations against Jerusalem to battle; and the city shall be taken, and the houses rifled, and the women ravished; and half of the city shall go forth into captivity, and the residue of the people shall not be cut off from the city [Zech. 14:2].

This is the last siege of Jerusalem, and it is not a pretty picture that is given to us here. The enemy takes the city, and when Zechariah says "all nations," I am of the opinion that he means that each nation will have representatives there. You might ask how that could be. Well, we have that same thing today with the United Nations. At the time that I am writing this, there are United Nations troops in Israel again. The soldiers come from different nations, and they more or less serve as a buffer between Israel and the enemy. It will be different in that day, but it will be an army that is made up of those who represent all the nations. They will come against Jerusalem, and they're going to take that city.

Again, let me give you Dr. Unger's translation. It is a sad state: "And the city shall be captured and the houses plundered, and the women raped, and half of the city shall go into captivity, but the rest of the people shall not be cut off from the city." Apparently, some will be able to escape. There are those, including myself, who believe that it will probably be the rock-hewn city of Petra to which they will go. Masada would also be a good place. That is where the Jews escaped to at the time of the invasion by Titus in A.D. 70. The only thing is that Masada would sure be a good target for bombers if they went there. I believe that the rock-hewn city of Petra could be the place.

This is a sad thing that is revealed to these people through Zechariah. The city is taken, the houses are plundered, and the women are raped. These are the three things that Zechariah mentions here.

> **Then shall the Lord go forth, and fight against those nations, as when he fought in the day of battle [Zech. 14:3].**

This is a picture of the Deliverer who is coming. It is at this time that their help will not come from the north or south or east or west, but their help will come from the Lord, the Maker of heaven and earth. This will be none other than the Lord Jesus Himself coming to the earth to deliver these people.

> **And his feet shall stand in that day upon the mount of Olives, which is before Jerusalem on the east, and the mount of Olives shall cleave in the midst thereof toward the east and toward the west, and there shall be a very great valley; and half of the mountain shall remove toward the north, and half of it toward the south [Zech. 14:4].**

"And his feet shall stand in that day upon the mount of Olives." This is a tremendous statement that is made here, and it is quite literal. The Mount of Olives is literal, Jerusalem is literal, these people are literal. When the Lord Jesus comes, His feet will stand upon the Mount of Olives. When Zechariah says His feet, he's talking about His feet, not His hands. Zechariah says that they will touch the Mount of Olives, and apparently he means that that's where the touchdown is going to be. I'm of the opinion that if men can send a missile that goes out to the moon and spends a few days there and comes back, and if they can put a battleship out in the Pacific and have that little capsule come down within two or three miles of the battleship, then God is not going to have any trouble with the Lord Jesus Christ touching down at the Mount of Olives. He is the glorified Christ today. He has nail prints in those feet, but those feet left the Mount of Olives when He left this earth, and He's coming back to the Mount of Olives when He comes again. This is exactly what was told His disciples. When He ascended, two witnesses came and said, ". . . Ye men of Galilee, why stand ye gazing up into heaven? this same Jesus, which is taken up from you into heaven, shall so come in like manner as ye have seen him go into heaven" (Acts 1:11). This is the fulfillment of it that will take place in the future. When? In the Day of the Lord, in the time when they are in great trouble, when Jerusalem has been besieged and taken for the last time.

"Upon the mount of Olives, which is before Jerusalem on the east." This mention of the east is not a casual statement. You will notice throughout Scripture that help for Israel is coming from the east. This is the reason they pay great attention to that eastern gate which some call the golden gate. I personally believe that the reference to the golden gate is the gate in the temple that shall be built. If you want to call it the golden gate, that's fine—it is the eastern gate. He will probably come in from the east.

Ezekiel also tells us that help is coming to them from the east. I think that it is interesting that we have been on the side of Israel from the very time that it became a nation—but we happen to be a *western* nation, you see. The real help for them is coming from the Lord, and there is no fulfillment of prophecy taking place there today. We can see that clearly when we put this prophecy down on what is going to happen.

"And the mount of Olives shall cleave in the midst thereof toward the east and toward the west, and there shall be a very great valley; and half of the mountain shall remove toward the north, and half of it toward the south." Great physical changes that are going to take place are mentioned to us here. There will be a great earthquake, and the Mount of Olives will be split right down the middle. Half of it will go to the north and half to the south.

"And there shall be a very great valley." Jerusalem today is surrounded by the roughest terrain that I know of anywhere. I frankly have been no place that can compare to it. It is rugged if you go north or if you go east or if you go south or if you go west—any direction that you might go. If you go south to Bethlehem, you would think you were riding one of the toboggan rides at Disneyland. Up and down you go—mountain after mountain—and it is rugged. If you go north, it is rugged. If you go west, it is rugged—big boulders and rocks. You've never seen such great big rocks. Going east down to Jericho—again, it is a rugged trip. The only thing is that the United States put in a wonderful macadam highway there. It is not a freeway, but it is a good highway, and it makes such an easy trip that the tourist doesn't realize what rough terrain it actually is.

> **And ye shall flee to the valley of the mountains; for the valley of the mountains shall reach unto Azal: yea, ye shall flee, like as ye fled from before the earthquake in the days of Uzziah king of Judah: and the LORD my God shall come, and all the saints with thee [Zech. 14:5].**

"And ye shall flee to the valley of the mountains." This is the reason that many commentators believe that they will flee over yonder to the rock-hewn city of Petra in the old country of Edom. However, we cannot be dogmatic because Scripture has not told that.

"And the LORD my God shall come, and all the saints with thee." This is a very interesting passage of Scripture. It is a picture of the Lord Jesus coming back to the earth. We find this also in Revelation 19 where we are told that the armies of heaven will follow Him. Here it says that all the saints will come with Him. Let us look for a moment at Romans 11:25 which says, "For I would not, brethren, that ye should be ignorant of this mystery, lest ye should be wise in your own conceits; that blindness in part is happened to Israel, until the fulness of the Gentiles be come in." This is the time of the fullness of the Gentiles when all the nations come up against Jerusalem. Romans 11:26 reads: "And so all Israel shall be saved: as it is written, There shall come out of Sion the Deliverer, and shall turn away ungodliness from Jacob." That time has definitely not come. The Lord Jesus' first coming doesn't satisfy this, and the Jews' present return to the land does not satisfy any of these Scriptures.

> **And it shall come to pass in that day, that the light shall not be clear, nor dark:**
>
> **But it shall be one day which shall be known to the LORD, not day, nor night: but it shall come to pass, that at evening time it shall be light [Zech. 14:6–7].**

There will be changes in the lighting of the earth. We are moving through that period of dawn to the coming of Christ to establish His Kingdom. This is, of course, a definite reference to the Day of the Lord, which is actually not a 24-hour day.

We come now to a new section in which we find the establishment of Israel's Kingdom here upon the earth.

> **And it shall be in that day, that living waters shall go out from Jerusalem; half of them toward the former sea, and half of them toward the hinder sea: in summer and in winter shall it be [Zech. 14:8].**

"The former sea" is the Dead Sea, and "the hinder sea" is the Mediterranean Sea. In other words, this will be a spring that will gush up water, and I think it means literal water. Apparently, Jerusalem, which has been an inland city, will suddenly become a seagoing city, that is, a port town. If you want to find in this verse a suggestion of the spiritual Water of Life, I think that will be true also because Zechariah also tells us that the Law, the Word of God, will go out from Jerusalem in that day. But this is literal water that Zechariah is talking about here.

> **And the LORD shall be king over all the earth: in that day shall there be one LORD, and his name one [Zech. 14:9].**

This is another very marvelous passage of Scripture. It refers to the Day of the Lord and to the fact that the Lord will be King—this is none other than the Lord Jesus Christ, of course. In that day there will be one Lord and one language. I'd like to turn to Zephaniah 3:9 which reads: "For then will I turn to the people a pure language, that they may all call upon the name of the LORD, to serve him with one consent." I do not think that we can be definite about which language this will be. God put up language as a barrier to mankind. No wall could be built any higher than the wall of a language barrier. That was the way in which He was enabled to scatter mankind and then, down through the years, to prepare for the coming of a Savior. Today the gospel is going back into those languages throughout the world. This is another of the great signs which indicate that we are moving toward the end of the age. There will be one language in that day, and I am going to be glad of that. I don't care what language it is, but everybody will speak that same language.

> **All the land shall be turned as a plain from Geba to Rimmon south of Jerusalem: and it shall be lifted up, and inhabited in her place, from Benjamin's gate unto the place of the first gate, unto the corner gate, and from the tower of Hananeel unto the king's winepresses [Zech. 14:10].**

This is very important as we are now looking at what is really the finale—this brings us to the end.

"All the land shall be turned as a plain [the Arabah]." The Arabah is the geographical name of that deep rift that comes down from above the Sea of Galilee, through the Jordan Valley, through the Dead Sea, down into the Gulf of Aqaba, and on into North Africa. It has been called the Great Rift. It begins at the Dog River at the coast north of Beirut in Lebanon. Zechariah is saying that there will be another great valley that resembles the Arabah.

Zechariah says that this great valley will go all the way "from Geba to Rimmon south of Jerusalem." This indicates the hill country of the ancient tribe of Judah to the border of Simeon on the south. It goes all the way from up north where Geba is located in the tribe of Benjamin to Rimmon, which is thirty-three miles southwest of Jerusalem. That will be a tremendous valley. All of that rugged terrain that is around Jerusalem is going to be smoothed out, and, apparently, Jerusalem will be elevated—"and it shall be lifted up."

"And it shall be lifted up, and inhabited in her place, from Benjamin's gate unto the place of the first gate, unto the corner gate, and from the tower of Hananeel unto the king's winepress." One commentator years ago said that this could not be literal because nobody could find the tower of Hananeel. The interesting thing is that archaeologists have since located it, and this brother is going to have to come up with another interpretation!

> **And men shall dwell in it, and there shall be no more utter destruction; but Jerusalem shall be safely inhabited [Zech. 14:11].**

This will be the first time in the history of Jerusalem that it will be a safe place to live. It is not so today, and it never has been. It is a very tender spot. The most sensitive spot in this universe is there. But when the Millennium has come, the Lord Jesus has come, His feet have touched the Mount of Olives, and these tremendous physical changes have taken place, then the people can dwell in Jerusalem safely. In other words, peace will have come to the earth for the first time.

> **And this shall be the plague wherewith the LORD will smite all the people that have fought against Jerusalem;**

> Their flesh shall consume away while they stand upon
> their feet, and their eyes shall consume away in their
> holes, and their tongue shall consume away in their
> mouth [Zech. 14:12].

"Their flesh shall consume away while they stand upon their feet."
This is a living death against the enemies of God that will take place.
The Book of Revelation tells us that this will take place in the Great
Tribulation period.

"And their eyes shall consume away in their holes [sockets], and
their tongue shall consume away in their mouth." May I say, this is a
terrible thing.

> And it shall come to pass in that day, that a great tumult
> from the LORD shall be among them; and they shall lay
> hold every one on the hand of his neighbour, and his
> hand shall rise up against the hand of his neighbour
> [Zech. 14:13].

That the enemy will be able to take the city will largely be due to this
tremendous revolution that apparently will be taking place in the city.

> And Judah also shall fight at Jerusalem; and the wealth
> of all the heathen round about shall be gathered to-
> gether, gold, and silver, and apparel, in great abun-
> dance.
>
> And so shall be the plague of the horse, of the mule, of
> the camel, and of the ass, and of all the beasts that shall
> be in these tents, as this plague [Zech. 14:14-15].

Jerusalem will become the commercial center of the world. We are
told elsewhere in prophecy that, just as they brought great wealth out
of Egypt in the days of Moses, they will bring great wealth into the
land of Israel when they return—that is, when God returns them.

We come now to a description of the Kingdom itself in contrast to the setting up of it. In the coming of Christ to the earth, He will put down all unrighteousness, all rebellion.

> **And it shall come to pass, that every one that is left of all the nations which came against Jerusalem shall even go up from year to year to worship the King, the LORD of hosts, and to keep the feast of tabernacles [Zech. 14:16].**

This verse means that there will not only be a remnant of Israel saved, but also a remnant out of each nation of the Gentiles. And they will be the ones who enter the Kingdom.

"Every one that is left of all the nations which came against Jerusalem shall even go up [that is, face in] from year to year to worship the King." They are going to face in to Jerusalem. There are great changes taking place at this time—not only physically, not only spiritually, not only economically, and in fact, in every area of life, but also the manner of witnessing for God will be different during the Millennium. Today we have been told, beginning at Jerusalem, to go to the ends of the earth (see Acts 1:8). Here we find that people from all nations are to go up to Jerusalem—that is what they did before the Lord Jesus came and died on the Cross. But after His death and resurrection He said, "Go to the ends of the earth with this message."

They shall "go up from year to year to worship the King, the LORD of hosts, and to keep the feast of tabernacles." The Feast of Tabernacles is the feast that the Israelites celebrated when they came out of Egypt. In that day, they will celebrate it because they have been brought from the ends of the earth back to Jerusalem.

> **And it shall be, that whoso will not come up of all the families of the earth unto Jerusalem to worship the King, the LORD of hosts, even upon them shall be no rain [Zech. 14:17].**

Someone will say, "I thought this was the Millennium!" It is, but the Millennium will be a time of testing those in this great multitude—a remnant, but a large remnant, I believe—who have turned to God. It is like being a church member—not all church members are Christians, by any means. Therefore, this period of the Millennium will be a time of testing.

> **And if the family of Egypt go not up, and come not, that have no rain; there shall be the plague, wherewith the LORD will smite the heathen that come not up to keep the feast of tabernacles.**

> **This shall be the punishment of Egypt, and the punishment of all nations that come not to keep the feast of tabernacles [Zech. 14:18–19].**

Egypt is used as an example.

> **In that day shall there be upon the bells of the horses, HOLINESS UNTO THE LORD; and the pots in the LORD's house shall be like the bowls before the altar [Zech. 14:20].**

"In that day"—Zechariah will not let loose of this expression!

"In that day shall there be upon the bells of the horses, HOLINESS UNTO THE LORD." Even a harness on a horse will be holiness unto the Lord. What does that mean? Everything will be for the service of God. The vessels in the tabernacle were called *holy* vessels. Why? They were unusual. I have a notion that after forty years in the wilderness they were beaten and battered, and I think they looked like they had really *had* it. But they were *holy* because they were for the service of God. And everything in that day will be for the service of God.

"And the pots in the LORD's house shall be like the bowls before the altar." Everything will be for the service of God then, but today we are living in a world where practically nothing is used for the service of God.

> **Yea, every pot in Jerusalem and in Judah shall be holiness unto the LORD of hosts: and all they that sacrifice**

shall come and take of them, and seethe therein: and in
that day there shall be no more the Canaanite in the
house of the LORD of hosts [Zech. 14:21].

"Yea, every pot in Jerusalem and in Judah shall be holiness unto the
LORD of hosts." Just think of that! That skillet that you have, the pot for
cooking beans or cabbage—in that day, all will be for the service of
God. Everything will be dedicated to Him.

"And all they that sacrifice shall come and take of them." Are they
going to offer sacrifices in that day? We read also in Ezekial that they
will. Certainly these sacrifices will look back to the death of Christ
just as the sacrifices before Christ looked forward to His coming.

"And in that day there shall be no more the Canaanite in the house
of the LORD of hosts." This means that all the hypocrites are going to be
removed. This means that every unbeliever will be removed, and
there will be none in the service of God unless they belong to Him.
This will be the Millennium, my friend. What a glorious picture this
is! This is a great finale and climax for the prophecy of Zechariah.

BIBLIOGRAPHY

(Recommended for Further Study)

Baron, David. *The Visions and Prophecies of Zechariah*. London, England: Hebrew Christian Testimony to Israel, 1918.

Feinberg, Charles L. *The Minor Prophets*. Chicago, Illinois: Moody Press, 1976.

Gaebelein, Arno C. *The Annotated Bible*. 1917. Reprint. Neptune, New Jersey: Loizeaux Brothers, 1971.

Ironside, H. A. *The Minor Prophets*. Neptune, New Jersey: Loizeaux Brothers, n.d.

Jensen, Irving L. *Haggai, Zechariah, and Malachi*. Chicago, Illinois: Moody Press, 1976.

Tatford, Frederick A. *The Minor Prophets*. Minneapolis, Minnesota: Klock & Klock, n.d.

Unger, Merrill F. *Unger's Bible Commentary: Zechariah*. Grand Rapids, Michigan: Zondervan Publishing House, 1963.

Unger, Merrill F. *Unger's Commentary on the Old Testament*, Vol. 2. Chicago, Illinois: Moody Press, 1982.